EXPLORING AMERICA'S

VALLEYS

From the Shenandoah to the Rio Grande

Prepared by the Special Publications Division
National Geographic Society, Washington, D. C.

EXPLORING AMERICA'S VALLEYS

Contributing Authors: TONI EUGENE, CHRISTINE ECKSTROM LEE, JANE R. McCAULEY, H. ROBERT MORRISON, GENE S. STUART

Contributing Photographers: RICHARD A. COOKE III, LOWELL GEORGIA, MARK GODFREY, DAVID HISER, TIM THOMPSON

Published by THE NATIONAL GEOGRAPHIC SOCIETY

GILBERT M. GROSVENOR, *President*
MELVIN M. PAYNE, *Chairman of the Board*
OWEN R. ANDERSON, *Executive Vice President*
ROBERT L. BREEDEN, *Vice President, Publications and Educational Media*

Prepared by THE SPECIAL PUBLICATIONS DIVISION

DONALD J. CRUMP, *Editor*
PHILIP B. SILCOTT, *Associate Editor*
WILLIAM H. ALLEN, WILLIAM R. GRAY, *Senior Editors*

Staff for this Book

RICHARD M. CRUM, *Managing Editor*
THOMAS B. POWELL III, *Picture Editor*
CINDA ROSE, *Art Director*
JODY BOLT, *Consulting Art Director*
ALICE K. JABLONSKY, *Senior Researcher and Assistant to the Editor*
BARBARA GRAZZINI, *Researcher*
TONI EUGENE, CHRISTINE ECKSTROM LEE, JANE R. McCAULEY, H. ROBERT MORRISON, LISA OLSON, GENE S. STUART, *Picture Legend Writers*
JOHN D. GARST, JR., VIRGINIA L. BAZA, PATRICIA K. CANTLAY, *Map Research and Production*
PAMELA A. BLACK, *Editorial Assistant*
CAROL ROCHELEAU CURTIS, *Illustrations Assistant*

Eroded sandstone formations guard a canyon near Sedona, Arizona, in the Verde Valley region.
PRECEDING PAGES: *More than two miles above ranch buildings in California's Owens Valley, the summit of Mount Whitney reaches higher than any other peak in the contiguous United States.*
HARDCOVER and PAGE 1: *In the Shenandoah Valley of Virginia, September brushes broadleaf trees with autumn color; January drapes a cabin, rail fence, and hillside in wintry white.*

JACK JEFFERS (PAGE 1); RICHARD A. COOKE III (PAGES 2-3); DAVID HISER (PAGES 4-5)

Pam Castaldi, Jennifer Woods, *Assistant Designers*
Engraving, Printing, and Product Manufacture
Robert W. Messer, *Manager*
George V. White, *Production Manager*
Mary A. Bennett, *Production Project Manager*
Mark R. Dunlevy, David V. Showers,
  Gregory Storer, George J. Zeller, Jr.
  Assistant Production Managers;
  Julia F. Warner, *Production Staff Assistant*
Nancy F. Berry, Mary Frances Brennan,
  Lori E. Davie, Mary Elizabeth Davis,
  Janet A. Dustin, Rosamund Garner,
  Victoria D. Garrett, Nancy J. Harvey,
Sandra K. Huhn, Joan Hurst,
Artemis A. Lampathakis, Katherine R. Leitch
Mary Evelyn McKinney, Cleo E. Petroff,
Sheryl A. Prohovich, Kathleen T. Shea
Linda L. Whittington, Virginia A. Williams,
  Staff Assistants
Jeffrey A. Brown, *Indexer*

ALASKA

Matanuska
Valley

Yukon

Mackenzie

CANADA

Fraser

Fraser Valley

Columbia

Snake

Upper Missouri Valley

Owyhee River → Jordan
Valley

Missouri

Star
Valley

North Platte
Valley

Kickapoo
Valley

Salt Lake
Valley

Platte

Steptoe Valley

UNITED STATES

Owens
Valley

Colorado

Verde
Valley

Arkansas

Arkansas
Valley

Gila

Middle
Rio
Grande
Valley

Mississippi

Rio Grande

HAWAII → Valleys of Kohala

MEXICO

Querétaro Valley

THE HAWAIIAN ISLANDS HAVE BEEN REPOSITIONED AND SHOW A LARGER SCALE

Oaxaca Valley

Saguenay Valley

St. Lawrence

Hudson Valley

Ohio

Shenandoah Valley

Wills Valley

Alabama

H avens for farms, cities, and factories, 20 valleys represent the many productive basins that cradle human achievement in America's mountain heights and prairie vastness. On the following pages the valleys labeled on this map offer contrasts in scenery, including a glacier-carved fjord in Canada, sunny fields from the Great Plains to southern Mexico, and fern-cloaked trails on the volcanic isle of Hawaii.

ARTWORK BY ROBERT HYNES

CONTENTS

Foreword	*9*
THE EASTERN HIGHLANDS	*10*
THE GREAT PLAINS	*46*
THE WESTERN UPLANDS	*82*
THE SOUTHERN REALMS	*118*
THE PACIFIC REACHES	*156*
Notes on Contributors	*196*
Index	*197*
Acknowledgments, Additional Reading, and Additional Music	*199*

Foreword

Valleys are corridors of our nation's history and havens of our heritage. Among the first valleys in the destiny of our restless country, the Rio Grande provided a passage for Spanish explorers venturing northward from Mexico in the 1500s, and on the eastern seaboard the Hudson Valley offered lands for settlement to Dutch and English colonists in the 1600s. A century later the Shenandoah of the Virginias served as a north-south throughway for travelers, and by the 19th century such overland routes as the Arkansas and the Platte in Nebraska pointed the way west.

While many valleys harbored Old World traditions, others cradled new customs. In the Appalachian wilderness and westward, many immigrants wed their European ways to life-styles influenced by the struggle to survive in the challenging environment of the American frontier.

Flowing rivers, scouring glaciers, and the uplifting and sinking of the earth's surface have all played a major role in creating valleys. Any natural elongated depression in the land—such as a gorge, a canyon, or a basin—qualifies as a valley, geologists say. Throughout America, rivers generally remain a conspicuous part of the valleys, adding scenic charm and attracting anglers, boatmen, and swimmers.

Often the rush of a river can distract a traveler's eye from other pleasing scenery in the area. As the following chapters reveal, between the river and the mountains there exists a world of surprising beauty inhabited by modern-day individualists. The valleys featured on these pages were chosen to represent varied regions and to offer a sampling of the many wonders awaiting discovery in thousands of valleys that grace America.

The adventures in this volume take you north to Canada, west to Hawaii, and south to Mexico. *From the Shenandoah to the Rio Grande* joins the title to suggest major climate and cultural differences found in many contrasting valley regions: the Shenandoah, a rain-blessed region where grain fields and apple orchards thrive and traditions stem from Europeans who crossed the North Atlantic; the Rio Grande, a sun-bright land where citrus groves tap the snowmelt of the distant San Juans and music on the airwaves carries the beat of the region's Hispanic pulse.

As the natural hearths of our civilization, valleys are often the destination in our travels and in our dreams. A free-lance writer recently noted that his thoughts keep drifting to the Shenandoah and its unhurried tapestry of white frame houses, red barns, and green rolling pastures. "Lately on my trips through the historic valley," he said, "I have been given to say, 'Put me down here for life, and I could be happy.'"

RICHARD M. CRUM, *Managing Editor*

In church at Isleta, New Mexico, Mabel Jojola wears a coral and silver cross necklace that blends Indian craftsmanship and Christianity, a faith brought to the middle Rio Grande Valley by the Spanish. Across North America and Hawaii many valleys conserve ethnic threads that brighten the fabric of life.

Fields and Forests:

THE EASTERN HIGHLANDS

Saguenay

In a new land mysterious with possibility, explorer Jacques Cartier found a people who believed that after life they would journey to the stars. They told him of a magical place called the kingdom of the Saguenay. Snow white whales splashed in the river that led to the kingdom. One moon's journey upstream, travelers passed lofty mountain walls and found towns that sprinkled a sweet land rich in rubies and gold.

Cartier learned of the kingdom of the Saguenay from the Huron Indians in 1534, while on a voyage of discovery down the St. Lawrence River through lands now part of the province of Quebec. He sailed past the mouth of the Saguenay River along the north shore of the St. Lawrence, but he never explored the kingdom's interior. The kingdom was a fantasy, but in a sense, a prophetic one. Except for the rubies and gold, the tales the Hurons told of the valley of the Saguenay would come true.

Almost everyone who came to settle in the valleys of the East had a dream. Many came before the Revolutionary War to make a new life in a new land. Venturing inland from coastal cities and towns, settlers often looked for choice valley lands with rich soils to farm, rivers and streams for water and transportation, and high sheltering mountains. A settler searches for a valley as a sailor seeks a harbor. In three seasons I explored four valleys in the eastern highlands: the Saguenay in the Canadian province of Quebec, the Hudson in New York, the Shenandoah of the Virginias, and the Wills Valley in northeast Alabama. Historically each of these areas has marked the edge of the frontier, and all have been avenues of trade, travel, and immigration. But as people put down roots, the lands gradually became stable pockets of life-styles brought from afar and homegrown in the valley.

> *Still French to their finger-tips*
> *in the midst of the vast lonely*
> *forest and the snow....*
> —from the novel *Maria Chapdelaine*

The culture and traditions of the Saguenay Valley are French-Canadian, pronounced with a resounding "oui!" Each year in the middle of the long Canadian winter, when deep snows pack the cities and towns along the Saguenay River and the sky and the land are the color of the moon, the people of the valley celebrate. The festival is known as Carnaval Souvenir, a carnival of remembrance. In February, residents from towns in the hundred-mile-long valley region, from villages along the St. Lawrence, and from faraway

Granite walls line Quebec's Saguenay Valley, a glacier-carved fjord whose river flows into the brackish St. Lawrence—one of Canada's major outlets to the sea.
PRECEDING PAGES: *Near West Point, New York, boaters at sunset enjoy the Hudson Valley and its river. Throughout the eastern highlands, valleys provided natural corridors that opened North America to explorers and settlers.*

settlements in the northern forest travel to the riverside city of Chicoutimi. They come to banish the gloom of winter in song, dance, and sport and to proclaim their Québécois heritage. When photographer Lowell Georgia and I arrived in Chicoutimi during Carnaval, we seemed to enter a fantasy world worthy of Cartier's claims. The town was dressed like a Christmas-card village, and people were elegantly attired in the latest fashions—of the 1880s.

"For 11 days the town is a theater of life as it was a century ago," explained Marc St-Hilaire, a young historian and director of activities for Carnaval. We talked about the Saguenay in the defrosting warmth of a small cafe, where we had escaped the 40-below-zero temperature outside. "It is a very small region, very far from everything. It is an oasis in the middle of the forest," Marc said. "The events of Carnaval allow everyone to understand their roots and to relive their history. To the people here, this is very important. Who are you if you have no sense of your heritage, if you do not protect it? If you preserve your culture, you preserve yourself. Otherwise, we are all the same, and we would be lost in the forest."

Between the forested hillsides and the river most of the Saguenay's 200,000 people live in villages and towns or in the valley's two largest cities, Chicoutimi and Jonquière. Pulp mills, aluminum plants, and hydroelectric dams throughout the area have replaced fur trading and forestry, the historic mainstays of the region. Exploitation of the timber resources surrounding the Saguenay attracted a few settlers to the region in the late 1830s. Some 150 years before that time the valley was considered part of the sprawling domain of the Hudson's Bay Company. The trading firm held exclusive rights to a land rich in beaver—the commodity prized in the prosperous fur exchange with the Indians. Just after the company's first lease ended in 1841, pioneers began arriving in increasing numbers; now most of the families in the region are descended from early settlers who came from southern Quebec to farm and to harvest the evergreen forests that roll to every horizon.

The heritage of furs and forests was displayed and reenacted throughout Carnaval. Men and women wrapped in long coats of beaver, fox, and squirrel strolled the icy streets. Many of those not dressed in the high city fashion of 1883 were clad in the heavy boots, tasseled caps, and red-and-black checked shirts favored by the lumberjacks: the men whose labor supplied the raw goods for the region's first industry.

One morning, under a high blue sky swept clean by winds from the Arctic, I stood with a crowd before the cathedral as the bishop of Chicoutimi said a prayer for several dozen lumberjacks gathered on the church steps. The event was a re-creation of a time gone by, when lumberjacks would set off for the woods at first frost—with the bishop's blessing—to work until spring. They would build temporary camps, steadily moving deeper into the forest, until the season ended and they returned home.

After the prayer the Carnaval lumberjacks tramped off to build their camp—in the middle of Chicoutimi—and I skipped through the city streets with a Pied-Piper parade of several hundred people, following a singing throng of woodsmen. If *joie de vivre* could melt the chill, Chicoutimi would have been balmy that day, but the air was so cold I seemed to breathe ice and exhale frost. When we reached the lumber camp, men were already at work, and in less than an hour they were enjoying a hearty meal of fresh fish, partridge, and rabbit beside a sturdy log cabin they had just built. "These men are made of this weather and this life," said my friend and guide Francine Ouellet. "The old way still lives in the minds of the people."

Throughout Carnaval the old way seemed as vibrant as the people enjoying it with humor and high spirits. At La Bonne Ménagère, a large building lined with indoor shops and food kiosks, I joined Francine and her husband, Serge Leblanc, a well-known community leader. We sampled meat pies called *tourtières*, maple candies, tarts plump with large blueberries—for which the region is famous ("It only takes one blueberry to make a pie," I heard)—and the Carnaval drink known as "caribou," a belly-warming mixture once made by adding alcohol to caribou blood. "Drink three caribous and you'll speak French!" Serge warned me.

Just as geographic isolation has shaped the character of the Saguenay's people, the current of cultural apartness has always flowed strong among the Québécois. Although movements for independence from Canada have failed in recent years, nationalist sentiments still run high. In the Saguenay, where people voted for separatism in more than double the numbers of the rest of the province, regional pride finds a special expression in the beauty of the French spoken. It is virtually the only language heard. One day Lowell and I drove along the river with our friend Diane Bouchard and her three-year-old son, Christopher. As we talked, in English, Christopher asked, in French, "Mama, are they pretending to speak English?" "No," Diane answered. "They are English-speaking people." "No," said Christopher, convinced. "They are only pretending."

People come to the Saguenay from all parts of Canada and the United States—and some from abroad—to study French at the region's two language schools, the Centre Linguistique in Jonquière and the École de Langue Française et de culture Québécoise at the University of Quebec in Chicoutimi. I talked with counselor Guy St-Jean at the Centre Linguistique.

"This area is a center of learning the French language because 95 percent of the population is Francophone," he said, "and because the French spoken here is so unaltered and pure. It is very close to the standard international phonetic alphabet." We looked at a map of the Saguenay. "This region was geographically isolated for so long that it became a linguistic island," he said. "Then in the 1920s and the 1940s, two large influxes of foreign workers arrived to build the Alcan plant and the Shipshaw Dam." Alcan's aluminum refinery in Jonquière is now the free world's largest. "The foreigners were quickly assimilated," Guy continued. "Just look in the phone book at all the foreign names. They all speak French now. The people who came here fell in love with the region, and I guess they fell in love with somebody else too—so they learned French. The land and people here are very beautiful."

I saw the beauty of the land and the river one summer day on a boat trip down the Saguenay. I was aboard the *Marjolaine II*, a ferryboat that cruises from Chicoutimi to the towering heights of capes Trinité and Eternité halfway down the river. From its source at Lac St-Jean the Saguenay plunges down to Chicoutimi, then deepens and widens as it flows eastward toward the St. Lawrence. Along the way it cuts through steep cliffs of Canadian Shield rock, cracked and worn smooth by ice and time and creased with imagined faces and creatures.

The Saguenay is a fjord, and its waters are tidal from its mouth at the St. Lawrence to Chicoutimi, 70 miles upstream. Along that stretch of river the fjord walls rise more than 1,500 feet, and most of the land looks as if Indians were still padding lightly through the woods. The forest is dark and mysterious; tall firs march up the craggy walls and trace the high crests of the fjord, like quills on a startled porcupine. Here and there, narrow streams that curl through the forest reach the cliffs and tumble to the river in veined waterfalls. Cruising down the Saguenay, I had the sensation of traveling through the heart of a great long mountain that had parted its walls for us to enter and glide along on its cool blue waters.

Edging the river, scalloped coves fringed with velvety green fields border sites where early pioneers settled in villages and where their descendants still farm the land and work in the forests. Anse St-Jean—cupped in the mountains along the Saguenay's south shore—is one of the oldest villages in the valley. Fields of buttercups, white daisies, and yellow mustard bobbed in the summer breeze as Lowell and I crossed a covered bridge and headed for one of Anse St-Jean's oldest farms—the homestead of Nazaire Boudreault. Ten years ago the Boudreaults opened their home as a "hospitality farm." Instead of checking into a hotel, visitors can stay with the Boudreaults. The guests can help with the chores or relax, as they choose. The practice is known in Quebec as social tourism, and it's popular with visitors who want to learn about the region through the life of its residents.

While Mr. Boudreault demonstrated the use of his horse-drawn plow, visitors watched his sister-in-law bake homemade bread in a traditional outdoor oven. I found Madame Boudreault seated in a rocking chair in her spacious kitchen. Two parakeets chattered in one corner, and in the heart of the house a century-old clock ticktocked a beat. "We live in a remote place, and the weather is hard," Madame Boudreault said. "In Anse St-Jean we must depend on each other, and that keeps the spirit of family strong. I think our guests feel that warmth, and that is why they return. Many people who come to visit us are from the cities, and their children think milk comes in plastic bags and eggs come in boxes. Here they can milk cows and go to the hen house and gather eggs, and they are enchanted."

Below Anse St-Jean the Saguenay appears unchanged since the time of Cartier. One blue and breezy afternoon Lowell and I left the village harbor aboard the fishing trawler *Gal*. Moving downriver, we scanned the waters in silence. We were searching for the belugas, beautiful white whales that swim up the Saguenay each summer to feast on salmon. The whales are thought to be a relic population, isolated from arctic beluga stock after the first glaciers retreated. Once they were hunted in the St. Lawrence by Indians and fishermen who came long before the first Saguenay settlers. Now they are protected—and admired.

In Ste-Marguerite's bay we spotted a spout and an arcing flash of white. Dancing whitecaps appeared to be everywhere. Suddenly we realized they were whales. Pods of shining belugas, mothers and calves, rose and rolled in the river, diving in double wheels, slapping their tails, creating illusions of ivory mermaids in a deep blue sea. They neared the boat, curious about us. I heard their high whistles and cries as they surfaced, *(Continued on page 22)*

Pig in the warm blanket of auctioneer Hervé Boudreault awaits the highest bid at Carnaval Souvenir. This winter festival, which includes livestock sales on the steps of the cathedral in Chicoutimi, celebrates the Saguenay heritage.

P etticoats swirl to the rollicking music of the cancan. At Carnaval,
Saguenay residents preserve their Québécois traditions by dancing to

French and French-Canadian songs, eating ample servings of tourtières—*meat pies—and ordering rounds of "caribou," a drink once made by mixing alcohol and caribou blood.*

Snowmelt waters tumble past a restored pulp mill at Val-Jalbert, a ghost town and park near Lac St-Jean—source of the Saguenay. Val-Jalbert prospered at the turn of the century when the construction of pulp mills began to transform the Saguenay Valley into a commercial region. Near the village of Anse St-Jean, Nazaire Boudreault and his son (opposite) work the land with a shovel plow—similar to the kind their forefathers used to break the Saguenay sod.

and I saw their pale eyes as they vanished below. We tapped on the hull, trying to lure them closer, but they frolicked farther into the river, leaving us behind. As we eased upstream, I looked back on the Saguenay's dark waters and watched the white splashes of the whales, diving with a beauty known to those who see them, whistling river songs for those who hear them.

Hudson

A *drowsy, dreamy influence seems to hang over the land. . . . The whole neighborhood abounds with local tales, haunted spots, and twilight superstitions. . . .*
—from *The Legend of Sleepy Hollow*

Just as French-Canadian traditions hold fast in the Saguenay, much of the spirit of New York's Hudson Valley echoes its early settlers, the Dutch. Less than 20 years after Henry Hudson sailed up the Hudson River in 1609, the Dutch began to settle Manhattan Island, soon establishing a thriving center of business and commerce that would later become New York City. To encourage settlement of valley lands up the Hudson, the Dutch West India Company granted large tracts of land, or patroonships, to entrepreneurs who would colonize the holdings.

"This patroonship system failed, but a concept of manorial land grants took hold under British rule in 1664," explained Nancy Gold of Sleepy Hollow Restorations. The organization owns and operates three historic sites located in the lower Hudson Valley.

"Two early manors are Philipsburg in North Tarrytown and Van Cortlandt in Croton-on-Hudson," Nancy said. "The creation of such large estates slowed development in the valley and kept much of the land along the river wild and uncluttered. But the manorial system of land grants did provide a means for many Europeans to come to this area and put down roots. We still have a lot of the old Dutch families and place-names here."

Even after the Revolutionary War, and into this century, the large-estate trend that started the Hudson Valley's development continued—with a wealth of variations. The mansions of the Roosevelts, Vanderbilts, Livingstons, Goulds, and studios of famous artists lined Hudson Valley shores from New York City to Albany. Today many of the homes are historic sites, magnificent monuments that present a lavish architectural fashion show of period styles and personal fancies.

I ventured into the brooding country just beyond Tarrytown to visit the fairy-tale home of 19th-century author Washington Irving. His house, known as Sunnyside, nestles in shady woods on the Hudson's eastern shore, by the place where the river widens so much the Dutch called it a sea—the Tappan Zee. Irving had converted a pre-Revolutionary Dutch farmer's cottage into a home that he described as "a little old-fashioned stone mansion . . . as full of angles and corners as an old cocked hat." Now restored, Sunnyside is a vision of whimsy and romance to charm the incurable dreamer.

In his Hudson Valley setting Irving created a new mythology of the New World with characters such as Rip Van Winkle, Ichabod Crane, and the Headless Horseman. Irving found enchantment and hauntings at every turn in the forest. He wrote of visitors to the valley, "They are sure, in a little time, to inhale the witching influence of the air, and begin to grow imaginative—to dream dreams, and see apparitions." As I walked in the damp cool woods around his home, dark eyes seemed to stare from the white bark of beeches. Rustlings in the trees sounded unnatural, sinister. It grew late and I quickly left the ominous woods.

From its source in the Adirondacks to its mouth just past Manhattan, the Hudson River cuts a 306-mile-long path from the wildest to the most developed site in New York State. The valley's heartland runs north from New York City to Glens Falls. When considered together with Lakes George and Champlain, the Hudson links New York State with Canada. This fact was not lost on the British or the rebelling colonists during the American Revolution. Both sides coveted the Hudson because it formed the best natural military route for the movement of men, food, and supplies to and from Canada.

"Control of the Hudson during the Revolution was critical to the Continental Army, and the river's defense centered on the fortifications here at West Point," explained Col. Roy K. Flint, chairman of the history department at the United States Military Academy at West Point. The academy is one of the most popular places in the Hudson Valley, not only for its picturesque setting on a riverside plateau in the Hudson Highlands but also for its significance as a Revolutionary War fortress and the site of the military academy. "The importance of this place has prompted some observers to call West Point 'the key to the continent,'" Colonel Flint said.

I sat with the colonel in his office, at a table papered with maps of the Hudson. He explained West Point's strategic value, pointing out forts, redoubts, and gun emplacements. At West Point the Hudson snakes through the walls of the highlands in a narrow S-shape; currents there are strong and tricky, and the winds can be treacherous. "I used to sail on this river; it's really a game trying to get through," Colonel Flint said. "There's no effective block of the channel until this point. With an iron chain and a wooden boom across the river to stop British ships, and with guns on both banks, the rebels must have convinced the British; the redcoats never tried to sail past West Point."

After the Revolutionary War the U.S. realized its need for professionally trained military officers and engineers. In 1802 Congress authorized the founding of the military academy at West Point. "All in all," Colonel Flint said, "the Hudson Valley has served us well."

> *Transported I am*
> *From the haunts of man*
> *On the banks of the Hudson Stream. . . .*
> —an old shantey

Across the Hudson from West Point I sat by a gazebo in the town of Cold Spring and joined in a popular summer pastime: watching the river. In the evening everyone in town seems to make a pilgrimage to the water. Boys skip stones; young girls whisper secrets; families picnic in the grass; old men exchange greetings; lovers seated on benches touch heads, making hearts. A

tugboat, its colored lights casting long beams across the water, churns up-stream pushing barges, and on the far shore a freight train click-clacks along, its low whistle moaning as it rounds the mountain and disappears. In all this activity a feeling of the valley's tranquillity prevails; it is the comfort of a town long lived in, the calm of a place well traveled.

Shenandoah

O Shenandoah, I long to hear you,
Away, you rolling river,
O Shenandoah, I long to hear you,
Away, I'm bound away,
'Cross the wide Missouri.
—old sea shantey

This haunting seafarer's refrain is a lyrical legacy befitting the beauty of the Shenandoah Valley of the Virginias. Folk music authority Alan Lomax interprets the words as "a call from the homeland . . . from the land itself, its rivers, and its familiar and loved hills."

The Shenandoah Valley has called many to a home on its land. A number of Indian tribes hunted, lived, and warred in the great rolling expanse. Legend holds that the name "Shenandoah" means "Daughter of the Stars." The Indians had long used the region as a trade and warpath route, and when the first colonists began to pour into the Shenandoah in the mid-1700s, they followed the old Indian trails down the broad green corridor, settling in to farm the rich valley soils.

Cradled between the Alleghenies on the west and the Blue Ridge Mountains on the east, the Shenandoah Valley extends for some 150 miles, from the region just south of Lexington, Virginia, north to the meeting of the Shenandoah and Potomac Rivers at Harper's Ferry, West Virginia. In between lies a paradise of farms, many worked by the same families for generations. In the northern valley huge apple orchards spread across the land, their trees frosted pink with blossoms in the spring.

Farther south, poultry and dairy farms checker a countryside where tall silos gleam silver in the sun and black-and-white cows graze in Irish-green fields. The mountains are always visible, and they seem to hold the valley safe from the world beyond. Often a pale haze circles the peaks, giving them an ethereal look, as if in a blink they might subside and roll back into the valley floor from which they rose.

The dense pathless forests and the steep basalt and granite cliffs of the Blue Ridge Mountains formed a barrier to westward expansion. Another ob-stacle was the forbidding wilderness that awaited pioneers once they had crossed the rugged Blue Ridge. Still, by the early 1800s, Scotch-Irish, Irish, English, and German travelers heading west from Virginia and south from Pennsylvania were steadily settling the valley. With the fertile bottomlands occupied, newcomers moved into the Blue Ridge Mountains. Pioneers cleared land, sold timber, trapped beaver and fox, and planted crops. But by

1900 much of the mountain soil was worn out from overplanting. Game grew scarce as more hunters filled the forests. Pinched between too many settlers and too little sustenance in a slow rural economy, people began to leave. Families too stubborn to give up eventually lost their farms to the Commonwealth of Virginia. After acquiring the properties, the state donated them to the federal government. The land became the Shenandoah National Park, opened in 1935. Today this public domain covers more than 300 square miles of sweeping vistas in the Blue Ridge Mountains.

In the 1930s there were virtually no bears in the park. As the forest has returned, so have the bears—on their own. Dan Carney and Nathan Garner, two graduate students from the Virginia Polytechnic Institute, are monitoring the Shenandoah's black bears to gather research data on their movements, reproduction, and population. In the spring Dan traps bears and attaches radio collars to the females, and Nathan tracks them electronically, plotting their wanderings.

For two days in May, I accompanied Dan on his daily rounds through the forest. Field technician Jim Stuart rode with us in an old pickup truck that was loaded with plastic tubs of raw meat—bear bait so ripe that not even the most curious soul would have dared to approach us. The first day Dan rebaited traps. We caught a wild dog. It rained continuously. After 14 hours and no bears we headed home. It rained again the second day. Then it hailed. The forest floor was a rich compost of leaves and logs, springy like an old mattress. We rebaited more traps, caught another wild dog, and told a lot of stories. As the day progressed, we discussed the intelligence of bears. With each empty trap my esteem for bears rose. By early evening I had pronounced them all Einsteins. Then it happened. At the most remote trap in the woods we found a bear tethered to a tree by the long snare around its foot. The animal was shiny black. As we approached, it shinnied up the tree, its powerful muscles rippling under its fur.

"Hi bear," Dan said. "Now settle down." Jim jabbed it with a syringe and injected a drug. Within three minutes the bear was asleep. While it dozed they tagged its ear, tattooed its lip for identification, measured it, and weighed it. "You're a healthy bear, aren't you?" Dan said. "Smile for old Dan." He checked its teeth to determine its age. "Now don't get too friendly with people. Some folks aren't very nice to bears."

> *Hurrah! Hurrah! For Southern rights hurrah!*
> *Hurrah for The Bonnie Blue Flag*
> *That bears a single star!*
> —Civil War song

Blood has stained the Shenandoah Valley, where today historical markers by the roads tell the story of battles in a land that seems too sweet for war. "Stonewall" Jackson confounded northern military leaders with his masterful Valley Campaign of 1862, but by 1864 the Confederacy was weakened, and the Union forces launched a last assault on the Shenandoah. *(Continued on page 35)*

FOLLOWING PAGES: *Meandering fog hugs the Shenandoah River in the Shenandoah Valley of the Virginias. Apple orchards and grain fields thrive on the rolling farmland, once trod by Indians, pioneers, and Civil War armies.*

D. CARY JACKSON

Weekend soldiers re-create a Union camp in the Shenandoah. Near the tents, bluecoats drill with bayonets (opposite) on the eve of the annual reenactment of the Battle of New Market.

FOLLOWING PAGES: *Confederates fire in mock combat at New Market, Virginia, where a corps of military school cadets—commanded by their professor—helped stall a Union advance in 1864.*

*Delicate sprays of
dogwood blossoms cheer
spring's arrival in the
Blue Ridge Mountains.
Sheltered by the
Alleghenies on the
west and the Blue Ridge
on the east, the fertile
Shenandoah Valley
lured settlers beginning
in the mid-1700s.
Latecomers moved into
the Blue Ridge foothills.
Fields worn out by
overplanting eventually
drove many settlers
away. The creation of
the Shenandoah National
Park in 1935 displaced
the remaining residents.
Today the regenerated
land offers quiet vistas
from forested ridges
above the valley floor.*

At the mid-valley town of New Market the troops of North and South clashed on May 15. The ranks of the outnumbered Confederates included a corps of 247 cadets from Lexington's Virginia Military Institute. The cadets, some only 15 years old, had entered service just days before. In the pitch of a rain-soaked battle the cadets surged to the front and helped stall the Union advance. This action was the Confederates' last tactical success in the valley.

The cadets' heroism is commemorated each year at the reenactment of the Battle of New Market, staged on the actual field of combat. I found the involvement of the participants in the reenactment as remarkable as the story of the conflict itself. From 17 states some 1,200 men and women, all wearing authentic uniforms and dress of the era, had gathered. They began to arrive Friday for the Sunday battle. Many would spend the weekend in camp, sleeping in canvas tents and living as Civil War soldiers lived.

Walking through the Union camp on Saturday, I passed groups of soldiers sitting around fragrant wood fires, drinking coffee, eating stew on tin plates, and telling stories. I felt like a stranger from another time. Ladies strolled by, their long calico dresses billowing in the breeze. On a broad green field, units of soldiers drilled in competition. Drumbeats and rolls split the air, and fife players piped the melodies of "Dixie" and "The Bonnie Blue Flag." The men refer to their groups as reactivated Civil War units. They pride themselves on the authenticity of their dress and the polish of their professional skills. "This is a whole subculture," said Brian Pohanka, historian for the 5th Regiment New York State Volunteers—a colorful unit known as Duryée's Zouaves. "A lot of the interest in reenactments began with the Civil War Centennial in 1965, and the level of authenticity and the number of participants have grown through the years.

"I'm a historian," Brian added, "and I want to know what it feels like to be a Civil War soldier. What it looks like, smells like, what it's like to camp on the ground. How can historians know what really happened if they haven't felt it? Reading letters written by Civil War soldiers, I find sentiments I can really sympathize with, like why the Union Army wasn't moving fast enough through the Virginia mud. Most people have the tendency to look at war not through the eyes of the soldiers who fought it, but through the eyes of the politicians who caused it. The soldier often knew better than anyone what was really taking place, and that's what we discover at reenactments."

Crowds cheered for both sides as Union and Confederate soldiers clashed in a frighteningly real play of war. Cannon thundered body-shaking booms; fire flashed from gun barrels; volleys of shots crackled like strings of firecrackers. Fallen soldiers darkened the ground. Sweeping scarves of blue smoke curled across the troops, and by the time the Confederates rushed uphill to capture the Union cannon, the battlefield was veiled in gray haze. From halfway through the battle until just after it ended, a hard rain fell. At some point during many of the New Market reenactments over the years, it has rained—just as it rained on May 15, 1864.

During the Civil War, plentiful rainfall nourished fertile fields of wheat and corn, which earned the Shenandoah the nickname "Breadbasket of Virginia."

Last light touches Harper's Ferry, West Virginia, where the Potomac River breaks through the Blue Ridge and meets the rocky shallows of the Shenandoah. A center of Civil War action, the town linked the east and the frontier west.

Of all the crops and produce grown in the valley today, the hallmark harvest is the apple. Just north of Winchester, the center of apple country, I visited the orchards of the D. K. Russell family. Five major varieties of his apple trees, including Red and Golden Delicious and Rome Beauty, cover 950 acres around Apple Pie Ridge.

Robert Russell, a gentle man in his 60s, walked me down the neat rows of trees, set against a rolling skyline of blue mountains to the west. "I can remember working these same trees with a horse and double shovel plow," Mr. Russell said. "Now we use tractors to cultivate, but we still pick all the apples by hand. Most of the orchards in this area are single-family operations. A few years ago there were too many growers my age, and I was worried about the future of the business. But now we've got a lot more young growers, and I'm happy about that. I believe we'll keep this valley going."

He paused and touched a tree branch. "The soil and climate here are just about perfect for apples," he said. "You need cool weather, but not extreme cold. We have good elevation, and the mountains protect us. The apple business is a lot of fun, but you've got to have the love of it. If you can communicate with that tree, if you can interpret all the signs that tree is giving to you, you'll be a successful fruit grower. And that takes a lot of love."

I Wills

'm in the heart of Dixie
Dixie's in the heart of me . . .
My home's in Alabama
No matter where I lay my head
My home's in Alabama
Southern born and Southern bred.
—from "My Home's in Alabama"

I was in the heart of waving country. Sometimes it's hard to concentrate on driving along the back roads of northeast Alabama, there's so much waving going on—from people in passing pickups and from people sitting on front porches, working in fields, or just walking along the road on a sunny June day. From the time I saw my first wave, I knew I was in the country of the real South, and I always waved back.

The part of Alabama waving country Lowell and I visited is known as the Wills Valley region. It extends for some 50 miles, from Valley Head near the Georgia border southwest to Gadsen. Just beyond Gadsden the 1,500-mile-long Appalachian Mountain chain—which begins near the mouth of the St. Lawrence River—tapers to an end in the low hills of central Alabama. Wedged between Sand Mountain on the west and Lookout Mountain on the east, the Wills Valley region stretches long and narrow, quiet and unhurried.

Wills was the boyhood home of Sequoyah. In the early 1800s this Cherokee developed a syllable-based alphabet that greatly increased the literacy of his people. The Cherokees became the first Native Americans in the present-day United States to use a writing system not based on a European alphabet.

Pressure for new lands for settlers prompted the U.S. Army to hasten the removal of the Indians. In 1838 Capt. John Payne came to Wills Valley and built a fort. The post became one starting point for the Cherokees' westward trek over the Trail of Tears. The route's name captures the sorrow of thousands of Cherokees who in 1838 were forced from their homes in southeastern states and escorted by federal troops to reservations in Oklahoma Territory. The army post, now known as Fort Payne, forms the business and population center in the heart of Wills. Mrs. Elizabeth Howard, a local historian, showed us around Fort Payne. "Agriculture has traditionally been the backbone of this region," she said. "Families here are close-knit and religious and proud of their roots. The church has always been a focal point of our life, and music has always been a strong part of our heritage."

This musical heritage is probably best expressed in the rousing success of a country-music band called Alabama. Three of the four members of the band, Randy Owen, Teddy Gentry, and Jeff Cook, are cousins from the Wills Valley region. They grew up singing rich gospel harmonies in church, and they appeared in small night clubs and at dances for ten years before achieving musical fame. In 1982 they became the first band to be chosen "Entertainer of the Year," the Country Music Association's highest award.

"These Alabama boys are the best thing that's ever happened around here," we heard time and again. Annually Alabama stages an outdoor concert in Fort Payne. In 1983 nearly all the proceeds—about $365,000—went to county charities. Lowell and I joined thousands of fans for Alabama's "June Jam." All day long people of all ages and from places as distant as Maine and Montana poured into Fort Payne's concert grounds. By the time the band came on stage in the evening, 40,000 people were on their feet roaring their approval for the songs Alabama sings of life in the Southland, the mountains, and the homespun past that made them who they are.

> *And we were leanin', leanin' on*
> *The everlasting arms of love*
> *Livin' all the simple joys*
> *This Dixie boy's made of.*
> —from "Dixie Boy"

The Alabama members learned to sing in the small country churches typical of the rural South, where voices lift gospel harmonies loud enough for heaven to hear. At the Beulah Baptist Church in Fyffe, a town on Sand Mountain, Lowell and I attended a traditional Sunday "singing." Voices of a hundred people blended with a simple beauty tender enough for tears: "*I once was lost, but now am found, / Was blind, but now I see.*"

Outside the church, singer Gus Smith said to me, "The Lord blessed me with a voice to sing, and I sing for one reason alone, and that's to praise God." Byron L. Reid told me, "We used to go down to granddaddy's whenever a new song book came out and sit around together and practice the songs until we got them just right." Carlos Bailey, whose three young children sang a lovely trio in church, explained, "We all grow up with singing here. It's a part of our inner being."

As in many churches in the valley, the hymnal music was printed in shape notes—squares, triangles, circles, and other symbols that represent each tone on the scale. These shape notes developed from a singing system of Shakespearean England and were brought to the colonies by early settlers. Traveling singing teachers used the shape-note system to help rural congregations learn to read music and to harmonize. Now, shape-note singing flourishes nowhere else in the world but in the American South, and northern Alabama is a key center of the tradition.

> *O-O-O-Oh!*
> *Sometimes it causes me*
> *to tremble, tremble, tremble.*
> *Were you there*
> *when they crucified my Lord?*
> —old spiritual

Gospel, spiritual, and shape-note singing differ from other forms of church music in the nature of the harmonies and the level of emotion expressed in the music. The harmonies of the Alabama band sound hauntingly like those we had heard at the church. "I think gospel is at the root of a lot of music," Alabama's lead singer Randy Owen told me. "Gospel, rhythm and blues, and country music are all heartfelt kinds of music. Even if you can't understand the language you can understand the feelings. We grew up in a settled, unsophisticated society that was pretty much at ease with itself. My daddy always felt that one way to bring people closer together was by singing. And he was right. I know that my mother and my daddy met by going to church singings. Everyone in my daddy's family can play a guitar, and my mother is a great pianist and singer. I think that a lot of people in this area are just born and bred to play music."

He talked of growing up in rural Alabama. He spoke in measured words, with a rhythm, like a song. "I don't miss picking cotton, but I do miss the atmosphere at harvesttime. I'd be out picking cotton, and I'd hear people singing some old gospel song, or some song that I'd heard all my life, and then I'd hear somebody else singing harmony with them as they'd pass each other picking rows, singing."

For inspiration Randy often goes to a quiet place above the valley on Lookout Mountain. "I know that I like to go out on Little River Canyon and just look, get ideas. There's a lot of natural beauty there that's pleasant, not loud. I love to sit out and listen to the katydids and all the night creatures. Just listen to the night. Listen to the night and see what it's talking about."

In the valleys of eastern North America, long explored, long settled, long known, I had found people who live close to the land, whose families reach back to the time when pioneers first felled a tree and broke the soil. They live on land their ancestors settled, but there is a difference now. The land lives in the people. Some, like Randy Owen, hear the music of the land and sing its lyrical words.

Listen to the night. To hear the voices that speak from the soil and to recognize that the language is yours is to know that the land is home.

Gothic country retreat, Lyndhurst belonged to railroad magnate Jay Gould.
The castle recalls a 19th-century era when industrial barons and statesmen built
riverfront mansions in the Hudson Valley from New York City to Albany.

*I*n the kitchen of the restored Van Cortlandt Manor in Croton-on-Hudson, Martha Wilcox prepares cookies from an 18th-century recipe. The baking demonstration is part of a living-history program that shows visitors how wealthy Dutch families lived in the valley during the late 1700s. Opposite: Mementos on the desk of Washington Irving include ornate Moorish knives. In this study at Sunnyside—his home in Tarrytown, New York—Irving produced his last work, a five-volume biography of George Washington. Irving achieved fame for his memorable tales about Rip Van Winkle, Ichabod Crane, and the Hudson Valley land he called Sleepy Hollow.

L*ife taps a beat to the strains of song in the Wills Valley region of northeast Alabama (opposite). On Sunday at the Beulah Baptist Church in Fyffe, singers (right) join voices to praise the Lord. At Gene Ivey's tire company in Ider, friends and customers listen as Bill Ott strums to Gene's lively fiddling (lower right). Gene built the fiddle—his tenth—in a workshop at the back of his store. "We just love to play," Gene says. "We do bluegrass, country and western, gospel—all the songs we learned living here in the hills and valleys of Alabama."*

Thousands of fans await the award-winning country-music band Alabama at concert grounds in Fort Payne, Alabama. Each year the band performs a "June Jam" and donates the show's proceeds to local charities. Three of the group's four members, including lead singer Randy Owen (below), call Fort Payne home. The "back-home, come-on music" of the performers and the plain-spoken appeal of their songs spring from the rural singing traditions of the Wills Valley region.

Windswept Corridors of

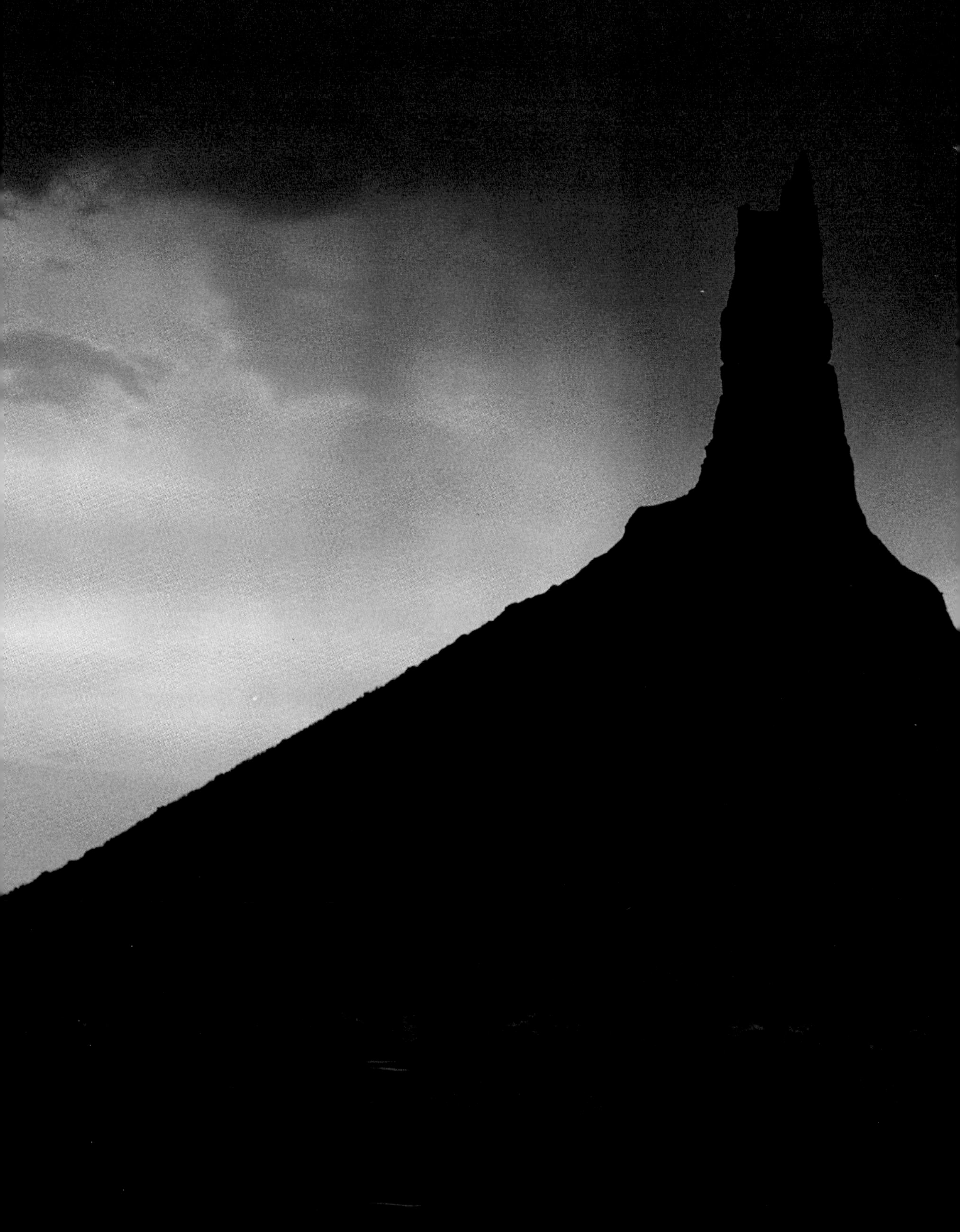

THE GREAT PLAINS

T Upper Missouri

he sound was like thunder, but the noon sky was filled with bright sunshine that summer day in 1805. Explorer Meriwether Lewis stopped walking and listened. Indians had told him about a "great falls" that roared. After a moment he moved forward again, carefully watching his step in the underbrush. Prickly pear cactus flourished in the area, with sharp spines strong enough to puncture deerskin moccasins.

As he emerged into a clearing on the bank of the Missouri River, the sight he saw left him dumbfounded. ". . . hearing a tremendious roaring above me I . . . was . . . presented . . . one of the most beatifull objects in nature, a cascade of about fifty feet perpendicular streching at rightangles across the river from side to side . . . at least a quarter of a mile. . . . the water decends in one even and uninterupted sheet to the bottom wher dashing against the rocky bottom [it] rises into foaming billows of great hight and rappidly glides away, hising flashing and sparkling as it departs."

Lewis would later write these words, but now his grand thoughts about the scenery were suddenly interrupted. Hearing a sound behind him, he turned. A huge grizzly had crept up on him. His best escape was the river, and he jumped into it. Apparently discouraged by the swirling water, the bear loped away.

Meriwether Lewis and William Clark, two army officers, had been commissioned by President Thomas Jefferson to explore the Missouri River and the lands acquired from France in the Louisiana Purchase of 1803. The river route they were following led them into a scenic wilderness known today as the upper Missouri Valley of Montana.

The spectacular cascade that Lewis and Clark had come upon was Great Falls, five chiseled ledges over which the river stairstepped. On both sides of the watercourse, herds of bison grazed in sweet tallgrass that waved across fenceless miles of prairie at the foot of the Rocky Mountains. Layers of fertile silt that once belonged to the Rockies nourished the lush valley. How the top skin of the mountains had been peeled off and spread across the valley floor involved changes that took place more than 250 million years ago. In that distant time, most scientists believe, today's continents formed a single landmass. Pressures intensified by heat deep inside the earth began to break the land block into crustal plates. The huge slabs started to drift, carrying the continents to their present positions.

Inching westward, the landmass that would become North America collided, perhaps as many as 50 times, with other moving chunks of land. Though occurring in slow motion over millions of years, the colossal bumping pinched

Sparkling cascade, Rainbow Falls drops the Missouri River at the western end of the upper Missouri Valley of Montana. In fertile valleys across the Great Plains, farmers produce a bonanza of grain, livestock, and dairy products.
PRECEDING PAGES: *A prairie storm gathers above Chimney Rock, a landmark that guided pioneers westward through Nebraska's North Platte Valley.*

MARK GODFREY (PAGES 46-47); DICK DURRANCE II (PAGE 48)

layers of earth, causing some of the layers to shift along fault lines and making others fold into high ranges.

The Rockies began rising to their jagged heights 67 million years ago. Some of the muddy streams that had lazily drained the nearly flat continent were now rushing out of the highlands, carrying rich debris. A great proportion—perhaps as much as one-half—of the Rockies' original top layer washed down and formed fertile layers of sediment across a broad basin, today called the Great Plains. Here in the nation's agricultural heartland I would explore four valleys, each a peaceful geographic counterpoint to the rugged ranges that wrinkle North America.

The upper Missouri Valley emerges from the shadow of the Rocky Mountains about a hundred miles west of Great Falls, the town named for the falls that had impressed Lewis and Clark. The valley curls eastward past isolated peaks and buttes and runs some 550 miles to the junction of the Missouri and Yellowstone Rivers, near the Montana-North Dakota border. This riverbed country has changed since Lewis and Clark camped here. Most of the roaring falls lie silently under deep waters bottled up by dams. The open grasslands where bison grazed now ripple with barley and golden wheat.

"I vowed I'd become a wheat farmer," Selmer Helland told me. I had met him at the home of his daughter and son-in-law, June and Dennis Bough, near Highwood, about 35 miles east of Great Falls. Selmer, at age 95, leaves most of the farming to Dennis and June. Through a picture window in their living room I could see the distant peaks of the Highwood Mountains. "I homesteaded with my family north of here on the highline," Selmer said, "just after the turn of the century. We were fortunate in that we had a steam tractor. During the slack season we could bring in a little cash by sodbusting for other settlers. But the conditions there weren't right for wheat. When I had the opportunity to buy land here along the Missouri, I jumped at it. Back then we grew one crop a year."

"It's not like that any more," said Dennis. "We plant two crops a year now. That keeps us busy. At harvesttime we can't push ourselves around the clock like some farmers who harvest for only a week or so. We have to save our strength because we'll be harvesting for nearly a month, even running all six of our combines. We're usually out of bed about dawn. We eat breakfast at 6:30 a.m., and we're at work by 7. We eat lunch in the fields. June cooks for the entire crew, maybe 15 men, and Selmer's job is driving the lunch wagon. We stop work about 9 p.m. and eat supper half an hour later. It takes us about 25 days to harvest some 8,000 acres of wheat and barley."

Outside the Helland farmhouse I surveyed this bountiful land. Montana calls itself Big Sky Country, an accurate description. With almost tangible weight the wide sky bends between far horizons. Frequently on late summer days the blue expanse breaks out in thunderheads, as rising heat roils off the hills and fields. Shadows of rain clouds move across the ripe land and brush against grain elevators. Occasionally a thunderhead will darken the threshold of a new type of man-made storage bin, the missile silo.

Along many roads in this sector of the valley, chain-link fences surround concrete circles, the openings of underground missile chambers. From each shaft protrude four banjo-shaped antennas. These devices pick up the slightest disturbance at the missile site, and a signal alerts military police from Malmstrom Air Force Base on the outskirts of Great Falls.

At Malmstrom a seat belt secured me in a chair at the control panel of a launch trainer. The instruments in front of me duplicated the missile controls that are manned continuously underground. My guide, First Lt. Norman L. Villanueva, pointed out the digital code wheels that could verify the command to fire. He emphasized safety precautions designed to prevent unauthorized firings, either accidental or deliberate.

"Even if all the secret codes match up correctly," he said, "the last step requires each of two men to insert his key and turn it. The keys must be turned within a second of each other, and the locks are 20 feet apart. It would be impossible for one man to set off a missile; two crews of two officers each must cooperate. We're sure these missiles can go off. We strive to be just as sure they won't go off accidentally."

The fireball of a bursting skyrocket scorched the night air. "Ooohs" and "aaahs" from a festive crowd mingled with fiery streamers curving earthward. It was Independence Day in Fort Benton, a riverside town in the upper Missouri Valley. Rain dampened many of the Fourth of July events, but the weather suited one activity—the frog-jumping contest.

Youngsters crouched over their frogs at the starting line. At the sound of the gun, they beat the ground with their hands, blew on the backs of their frogs, did almost anything to coax their laid-back jumpers across the finish line. The antics of the event had changed little from those in the famous short story that had inspired the competition. Mark Twain had written "The Celebrated Jumping Frog of Calaveras County" during the gold-rush days of the frontier. Fort Benton claims a large share of that era's lusty spirit. In the mid-1800s the town was a busy trading post for fur trappers and miners. Steamboats unloaded thousands of tenderfeet eager to get to Helena and Virginia City and other remote gold camps in western Montana.

"We are at the moment passing some of the most unique and imposing scenery I ever saw," a riverboat passenger observed in 1866 as he steamed through the valley toward the head of navigation at Fort Benton. "Great jagged towers, pinnacles and ramparts rise out of the long ranges white and grand. White sandstone is the rock. Palisades circle around detached bluffs like pillars against their sides with rounded capitals. One immense rock like rusty iron rises from white battlements of a great fortress . . . . Detached columns like monuments . . . look solemnly . . . while fretted and corrugated walls seem gothic in their architecture." The diarist was describing the White Cliffs region. Today this section of scenery lies within a 150-mile stretch of river that is part of the nation's Wild and Scenic River System.

From Fort Peck westward toward Fort Benton, the Missouri Breaks—a natural display of grotesque columns and ridges along the river—exhibit nature's sculpting power. This area, once a high plateau, stood in the path of a glacier pushing southward 750,000 years ago. The ice sheet chewed into the plateau and created Montana's Little Rockies, the Bear Paws, and the Highwood Mountains. In the same slow sweep the glacier relocated the upper Missouri Valley by cutting off its river. The Missouri originally flowed from Great Falls northeast to present-day Havre, then *(Continued on page 56)*

FOLLOWING PAGES: *Gnarled by the ceaseless flow of the river and centuries of wind and rain, a landscape known as the White Cliffs encroaches on fields striped with wheat and barley in the upper Missouri Valley.*

Grain elevators dominate Carter, Montana. The chores of harvesting wheat and pitching hay no longer require tens of thousands of farm workers. Today modern machinery—such as the huge cultivator being serviced by mechanic Dennis Lorang (opposite, foreground)—enables two or three hands to work farms as large as 2,500 acres. In the last 60 years improved equipment and fertilizers have helped Montana farmers boost wheat production fourfold.

eastward, where the Milk River now runs. Blocked by the ice field, the Missouri had to find a detour. By the geologic calendar, the river wasted little time. It dropped south about 60 miles and began to carve its present course. Over the centuries, with the assistance of wind and rain, the Missouri fashioned the bizarre beauty of the Breaks. This wilderness in the valley of the nation's longest river echoes some of the natural wonders of the Kickapoo—a river corridor in Wisconsin where I had begun my valley odyssey.

Kickapoo

It's hard to find a long run of level ground in the Kickapoo Valley. This land in the southwestern corner of Wisconsin displays a craggy face lined with hills. Yet a gentleness pervades the area. Oak, maple, basswood, and hickory stipple the slopes and seem to soften the terrain. Limestone-capped bluffs and outcroppings of sandstone break the valley's soft harmony along the Kickapoo River. "Kickapoo" comes from an Algonquian Indian word, its true meaning unknown. From folklore comes one interpretation: "He who goes there, then here." Today's residents of the valley—who call themselves "Kickapoogians"—say the word means "crooked river."

The watercourse winds under rock shelves, dodges moss-covered cliffs, and threads tunnels of elm and silver maple. In its 125-mile plunge to the Wisconsin River the Kickapoo drops 350 feet, but never in wild jumps. It always flows in gentle hops and runs. The valley that the river has carved over many centuries forms the longest and deepest depression in a zone geologists call the Driftless Area.

I learned the origin of the name from Ron Nelson, superintendent of Wildcat Mountain State Park, near the northern tip of the valley. "A huge glacier covered most of the state about 18,000 years ago," Ron said. "When it began to advance southward, it scoured the land like sandpaper, crushing huge boulders, snapping natural rock bridges, scraping soil from hilltops, and smoothing out most of the surface.

"Thick layers of sediment deposited by the glacier formed kettles—steep-sided hollows that blocked drainage, creating the thousands of lakes you see today in northern Wisconsin. But most geologists believe that the glacier didn't reach this corner of the state. The land here is rough, with sheer ridges and deep valleys. That's because this area escaped the great scouring edge of the glacier. We don't find here the usual telltale drifts of sand and rock left by a melting glacier. That's why we call these lands the Driftless Area."

Living legacies of the region's glacial past survive in a number of relic species of plants that bloom here, far from their original habitat. Along the upper valley I had passed remnants of such vegetation, notably hemlock. On Razorback Ridge, near the top of Wildcat Mountain, Ron pointed out a dozen blossoms of pasqueflowers. They stood about six inches high, raising white star-shaped blooms about the size of a half-dollar. "The normal habitat of these relatives of the anemone," Ron said, "is the cooler climate of the Rocky Mountains and northern Great Plains. You can even find species of arctic plants here in the valley.

"These species are here because millions of years ago their northern ancestors migrated southward ahead of the advancing glaciers. The Driftless Area, being free of ice, was an inviting place for the plants to take root. Succeeding generations of these species have survived here mainly because of the river. Mists from the Kickapoo cool the plants in summer and help provide moisture that the plants need."

As the last glacier began to recede, man joined plants and other animals in the Driftless Area. The early inhabitants, about 10,000 years ago, were hunters armed with crude spears. Many centuries later, in the 1600s, the demand for fur animals lured French trappers into the valley, where they traded with the Kickapoo Indians who lived there. The settlers who arrived in the 1840s cleared farm tracts in the virgin forests, and agriculture became and remains the economic base of the Kickapoo Valley.

One group of early settlers—the Norwegians—began farming the high hilly country around the town of Westby on the northwestern edge of the valley. As I approached the town, hospitable signs proclaimed *Velkommen til Westby*. Each spring the residents celebrate their Norwegian heritage with a festival called Syttende Mai—17th of May.

"It's the Norwegian version of the Fourth of July," explained Mrs. Thora Holden, president of the festival and a descendant of Norwegian immigrants. "The countryside here appealed to the early settlers. It gave them at least some feeling of their homeland, although the hills of Norway are higher and its valleys are steeper and narrower than here. The newcomers settled in the valley and tried to live much as they had in the old country. They worked hard, and they thrived."

On the Saturday evening of the festival, a concert featured Erik Bye, a Norwegian television personality. "The language here is most interesting," he said, while waiting for his performance to begin. "It's not just that so many of the people still speak Norwegian. It's more that local dialects now dying away in Norway have been retained. I believe it shows how isolated the early farming communities here must have been."

One sun-dappled morning as I drove southwest of Cashton, I spotted a plowman working a team of six draft horses. I pulled over to the side of the road. The farmer turned the team at the edge of the field and stopped. He pulled a bandanna from his pocket, mopped his brow, and smiled. "Beautiful morning," he said. He explained that he rested his team at the end of each furrow. "It takes a little longer, but you have to consider the animals too. And it gives a person a chance to think."

This wisdom, profound in its simplicity, belongs to the Amish. Families of this religious sect have settled in the northern part of the valley. Their faith, based on Puritan tenets espoused by a 17th-century Mennonite elder, frowns on the use of electricity, automobiles, and tractors. A skillful mix of brawn and brains has made the Amish some of America's most productive farmers.

Farther down the road I called on William Kempf, one of the valley's most industrious Amish farmers. On his place northeast of LaFarge, no hands remain idle for long. The barn, silos, shops, the house, everything was built or renovated by the Kempf family. Of Mr. Kempf's 14 children, three farm their own land in the Kickapoo Valley, and a daughter lives on an Ohio farm. The ten children still at home pitch in with the cooking, cleaning, sewing, gardening, and fieldwork and help care for the cattle, horses, and pigs.

Although Mr. Kempf doesn't rely on electricity and owns neither a tractor nor an automobile, he can use diesel engines to power his cabinetmaking shop and his sawmill. "Amish leaders in each community decide which modern conveniences are acceptable," he explained. With the trimmings and slab-wood from the sawmill lumber, he fuels fires for the maple syrup he produces. Sapping season lasts no longer than three weeks in late winter or early spring. The days must be warm, the nights cold. It's this rise and fall in temperature that starts the sugar-maple sap flowing.

"It's important to boil down the sap the same day it's collected," Mr. Kempf said. "If you let it sit, even overnight, it gets stale. That gives the syrup a strong flavor with a trace of bitterness; it doesn't turn out mild and delicate as maple syrup should."

Many acres of rich Kickapoo soil lie in pasturage where the land is too steep for cultivation. But even on level land not all farming ventures in the valley have succeeded. Occasionally I passed vacant farmsteads sitting in decay, a sharp contrast to the valley's well-tended farms.

"You'll find the same trend here as you would find in most any agricultural community. There just aren't nearly the number of farms here there used to be," Bernard Smith lamented. Mr. Smith has spent all his 72 years on farms in the Kickapoo Valley. "Many of the smaller family farms have been consolidated," he said. "As farm machinery improved, fewer people were required to work the land. Nowadays most of our children grow up and move away. Of course there are those who will remain to help on the family farm or to settle down on a farm of their own. But it's going to be much harder than it used to be because of the high-priced machinery and high interest rates."

Ingenuity has helped Kickapoogians overcome many obstacles. In the lower part of the valley, for instance, the people of Soldiers Grove came up with a plan to improve their town and at the same time save it from the annual flood-waters of the Kickapoo. They moved their business district into new buildings on higher ground and became one of the nation's first communities to tap the energy of the sun. Solar energy furnishes at least 50 percent of the heat used year round by the town's commercial buildings, including a supermarket, a health clinic, and a bank.

I found another example of Kickapoogian enterprise between the towns of Elroy and Sparta, where the Chicago and North Western Railroad once ran. The closing of the line in 1964 led to the opening of an innovative bike trail. A year after the last North Western locomotive thundered over the tracks, the Wisconsin Department of Natural Resources bought 32 miles of right-of-way between the towns. A smooth surface of crushed limestone replaced tracks and ties, and in 1966 the railroad bed became an official bike path.

The grade of the trail slopes no more than 3 percent. I was glad of that as I pedaled a ten-speed bike along the course. I wheeled through a blend of beauty: rolling hills, wooded slopes, clear brooks shadowed with trout, ponds rippled by muskrat, marshes dotted with cattails and red-winged blackbirds. The scenery vanished when I followed the path into one of the three tunnels that bore through huge hills. Most riders carry *(Continued on page 69)*

In skunk-skin hat and beaded buckskin, "Wild Bill" Steffensmeier rams home the lead ball in a muzzle-loading rifle. He helps bring the days of the wagon scout to life for visitors along the Oregon Trail in Nebraska's North Platte Valley.

Yellow-spine thistle captures the sunlight in a North Platte Valley pasture. The familiar sight of the bristling plant and the song of the western meadowlark (right)— Nebraska's state bird—have prompted Nebraskans to say: "When you see the thistle and hear the meadowlark, you know you are home."

FOLLOWING PAGES: *In the Arkansas Valley low-lying fields border the river that shaped the valley. The corridor produces soybeans and grapes and supports light manufacturing plants and cottage industries.*

D ocket of doom for lawbreakers notes trial dates in the once-feared court (opposite) of Isaac C. Parker, the Hanging Judge. In the 1800s Parker presided in Fort Smith. His jurisdiction included Indian country, an outlaw-plagued region that covered most of present-day Oklahoma. The jurist befriended many of the people he had convicted and found jobs for some. He acquired his nickname by sentencing 160 defendants to death by hanging. Barred windows (below) identify the new jail wing built in 1889 to replace the crowded cells under Parker's courtroom, today restored as a National Historic Site.

flashlights and walk their bikes through the long dark passages. Inside, the hush of blackness surrounded me, and I tried to imagine the clamor of locomotives that once shook these stone walls. In past years as many as 50 freight trains a day rumbled through the tunnels.

Many bikers view the Elroy-Sparta Bikeway as a course for physical conditioning. I saw it as a healthy example of the human spirit. Kickapoogians had helped turn the loss of a railroad into the country's first bike path recognized by the U. S. Department of Interior as a National Recreation Trail. The early homesteaders who developed the valley had displayed similar resourcefulness. Self-sufficiency is a tradition in the Kickapoo, and in the strength of this resolve lies the future of the valley.

Arkansas

Unlike the narrow, twisting Kickapoo, the Arkansas Valley begins to fan out into a rolling floodplain between the north face of the Ouachita Mountains and the south slopes of the Ozarks. The heart of this lowland extends from Fort Smith on the Oklahoma-Arkansas border to Morrilton, Arkansas.

Bluffs clad in oak, hickory, and shortleaf pine edge the flat valley and its river, the Arkansas. Though the erosive power of this meandering stream helped shape the region, similar violent forces of nature that forged the Rockies molded the highlands that became the Ouachitas and the Ozarks. The massive uplift of the Ouachitas weathered out in long east-west ridges. Major streams, cutting across these ridges rather than flowing along them, created spectacular cataracts. Such plummeting beauty enhances Petit Jean, a flat-topped mountain cleft by a canyon.

An appointment prompted me to leave the valley floor and head for the top of Petit Jean. The mountain takes its name from the heroine in a romantic legend about a French sailor. When he set sail for the New World, the story goes, his sweetheart boarded his ship disguised as a cabin boy—Petit Jean— and stowed away to America. Her ruse was successful, but she died of a fever shortly after arriving in the Arkansas Valley. A grave marker with her name stands on the brow of the mountain.

The site overlooks a valley vista that I found memorable this particular spring day. Far below on the floodplain, cattle grazed in fields bright with clouds of yellow cinquefoils. Along the sweeping curve of the Arkansas River tugs pushed strings of barges. In the distance Mount Nebo commanded a 1,775-foot-high view of Lake Dardanelle, a 34,292-acre body of water sprawling behind a dam on the river. To the north rose the state's tallest peak, Mount Magazine—2,753 feet high. Petit Jean, Magazine, and Nebo are all products of the Ouachita creation.

In 1953 Winthrop Rockefeller moved to the summit of Petit Jean. Before serving two terms as governor of Arkansas, he devoted his energies to his

"I quilt by the piece," says Edna Seeman as she deftly stitches a pattern known as the Double Wedding Ring. Edna and others in the Arkansas Valley sell their crafts nationwide with the backing of a rural marketing outlet.

mountaintop farm. Upon his death in 1973 his estate provided for the establishment of a foundation dedicated to the easing of world hunger through animal husbandry. Today that institution, Winrock International, occupies many of the buildings of the former Rockefeller farm.

Inside the complex I met with Dr. Jim Yazman, an animal scientist seeking ways to increase production and profits from animal grazing. He stresses the wisdom of raising goats instead of cows. "You can buy several goats for the price of a single cow," he told me. "This means that if one of your animals dies, you will still have a herd large enough to prevent your entire operation from being wiped out. Also goats don't require as much feed as cattle; they can produce milk on sparser browse-covered grazing land.

"Most people aren't used to thinking of goats as good sources of milk and meat. That's probably the most difficult obstacle to overcome in getting goats widely accepted on farms both here and overseas. But we've found that farmers quickly grow enthusiastic about goats once they try raising them."

The challenge of making small woodlots profitable takes up much of the time of Dr. Evert K. Byington, a range scientist at the foundation. "A surprisingly high percentage of woodland exists as relatively small plots owned by individual farmers," he told me. "As world population continues to grow, we're going to need more wood for fuel, for building material, and for making paper. Our needs may outgrow the capacity of our traditional lumber resources—the national forests and the private timberlands owned by large corporations. If we can use smaller woodlots efficiently, we'll be able to delay running out of wood products. And we'll increase the incomes of many good farmers whose limited operations don't qualify as big business."

Enhancing individual effort to increase productivity and profits is a practice hard at work in the Arkansas Valley. Since early settlement days people in this region have made and sold crafts valued for their quality workmanship and painstaking detail. Near the town of Dardanelle I found craftsmaking organized into an industry.

"Our crafts company—one of the few in the United States that's breaking even financially—teaches crafts that people can do in their own homes. We furnish designs and materials, and we buy the finished items, such as dolls, baskets, and quilts, from the workers. We sell these products through our own local retail and wholesale outlets located nationwide." Speaking was Lou Vitale, a tall man in his mid-40s. He had founded ARVAC Rural Folk Crafts as part of his job as the economic development director for the Arkansas River Valley Area Council (ARVAC), a community action agency.

"Our biggest problem is isolation," he continued. "Our producers are spread out through eight counties across 5,000 square miles in the valley and surrounding hills. There's virtually no public transportation. Some of our Vista volunteers drive a hundred miles in a single day to recruit and train craftspeople and help them market their work. Our efforts are paying off. The craft products are popular with buyers, and we've been able to help some of our producers become self-sufficient."

In the Ouachita and Ozark Mountains I met some of ARVAC's artisans and the items they fashion. Rene Soderling, a young woman with short blond hair proudly told me that one of her designs for her Happy Face Clown dolls had been chosen by ARVAC to be produced for market. Chet Austin showed me how to split off even strips of oak with a drawknife. Then he introduced me to

the skill of weaving the strips into sturdy baskets. Madge Powers and her granddaughter, "Sam" Salmon, brought out stuffed dolls that stand three feet tall. Each doll will merrily follow the steps of any youngster who slips his or her dancing feet into the doll's foot straps. Edna Seeman invited me into her home and displayed the exquisite quilts that she sews for sale.

Quilting is also a social function for Edna. Once a week she joins a few of her neighbors for a quilting bee. They meet in a vacated schoolhouse a short walk from Edna's home, located north of Lamar in the Ozarks. She took me to the building and showed me one of the most beautiful quilts I have ever seen. It stretched across a large frame and featured eight-pointed stars of red and blue diamonds sparkling against a creamy white background.

Not all craftsmen in the valley work for ARVAC. In Russellville, across the river from Dardanelle, I met "The Arkansas Knifesmith," a gregarious tradesman in his early 50s. "I made my first knife before I was ten," Jimmy Lile told me. "Whittled it out of wood, blade and all. In 1970 I decided to go into the knife business full time. I figured it would take four years before I started breaking even. Then a magazine featured me and my knives. In just ten months I was making a living."

He took me into his sales room and opened a display case. "Of the larger models, this one is the most interesting," he said. "It's a survival knife. I developed the idea for it when I was thinking one night about the kind of tool I would want to have with me if I was ever in a plane crash." The knife measured 14 inches. Its pointed blade curved slightly. Heavy green cord was wrapped around its metal handle. Along the back of the blade a set of razor-sharp teeth formed a saw blade.

"There's a compass in the hollow handle, which also has a waterproof compartment for matches and other survival items," Jimmy said. "The wrapping on the handle is nylon fishing line; it can be unwound for catching fish or making snares. This knife will punch through the fuselage of a plane, enabling you to escape even though the doors are blocked."

"Why would anyone pay a hundred dollars or more for a knife, when factory-made ones are available for much less?" I asked.

"For three reasons," Jimmy replied. "First, a handmade knife is easier to use. It fits the hand, and it holds its edge. Second, a handmade knife has refinements, such as the fit of the handle to the guard and the guard to the blade. This gives the knife aesthetic appeal and lasting design. And third, most knifesmiths will make a knife to a customer's design."

Since 1970 Jimmy has made hundreds of knives, ranging from pocket-size blades to sabers. Advertised mainly by the praise of satisfied customers, Jimmy's knives sell throughout the world.

One of the first men in the Arkansas Valley to make a name for himself was Isaac C. Parker, the Hanging Judge. Parker held court in Fort Smith a century ago. On the Arkansas border, which separated the state from Indian country, the fort quartered soldiers who worked to keep the peace among the Indians and between them and the white settlers. Desperadoes trying to escape federal marshals by slipping into the Indian region often stumbled and

FOLLOWING PAGES: *After an early morning milking, Holsteins exhale clouds of vapor in Wisconsin's Kickapoo Valley. The area's fields of alfalfa benefit from subsurface layers of limestone rich in calcium—a natural plant food.*

landed in the courtroom of Judge Parker. His determination to carry out the letter of the law terrified the most cold-blooded outlaws. One defendant, objecting vigorously to testimony against him, was admonished by Judge Parker: "You'll have your turn and justice will be done."

"That's what I'm afraid of," the defendant cried.

"It was not surprising that he gained so much notoriety," National Park employee Guy Nichols told me. "During his 21 years on the bench, Parker tried more than 13,000 people. He sentenced 160 of them to hang; 79 went to the gallows. These numbers show how tough his job was. He was responsible for enforcing the law not only in western Arkansas but also throughout Indian country, an area that covered most of present-day Oklahoma."

Despite his fearsome reputation, magnified by sensational newspaper articles, Judge Parker fought for reforms. He campaigned to replace squalid, often overcrowded prison cells, a fight he won after ten years. He sentenced young offenders to serve time where they could learn a trade, then he wrote letters of recommendation for them to prospective employers. He served on the local school and hospital boards. After he died in 1896, one newspaper eulogized the " . . . bold and fearless stand taken by this magnificent . . . jurist, when Crime stalked red-handed and relentlessly through the country over which he had judicial sway."

Fort Smith was never completed as a military outpost, but the station did become an important supply base for gold seekers headed for California. Confronted by the Ozarks and the Ouachitas—the only major mountain barriers between the Appalachians and the Rockies—many migrating miners sidestepped the heights by following the Arkansas Valley to Fort Smith. Valleys had become the natural highways to the golden west. Of all the river-graded routes, one of the most heavily traveled was that of the North Platte.

North Platte

"Wagons Ho!"

The command split the quiet summer morning like a rifle shot across shallow water. Lines snapped, horses leaned into well-oiled harnesses, and my prairie schooner lurched forward. I had joined an Old West wagon train near Bayard, Nebraska, a farming community about 40 miles east of the Wyoming border in the North Platte Valley. Wagonmaster Gordon Howard and his wife, Patty, assemble their covered wagons four times a year for short trips that give paying guests a chance to experience pioneer life.

Forty of us had signed up for the trail adventure. The day before we left, Gordon—a man with a great gray-streaked beard—had outfitted us with authentic western gear. We drew our blue-speckled enamel mugs and plates, cutlery, and white muslin duffel bags for personal belongings. Tents and the covered wagons would shelter us at night. There was traditional work to be done before our six prairie schooners could roll. While the women sewed sunbonnets, I helped a group of men prepare the wagon wheels. We loosened the axle nut, jacked up the wagon, slid each wheel part way off its fixed axle, and daubed a glob of thick black grease inside the wooden hub. I learned that the pioneers had used a sticky mixture of pine tar and lard for axle grease. It was carried in a bucket hung at the back of each wagon. If the bucket ran dry, the pioneers would make grease from the fat of bison and other prairie animals. Even the hooves of the oxen pulling the wagons were greased, then wrapped in bison hide to provide protection against "foot evil," a disease animals contracted by trudging too long through mud.

In the 1840s single trains of sometimes a hundred or more covered wagons rattled up the North Platte Valley. It took these "mobile communities" as long as five months to reach Oregon from Missouri. As in any group banded together for a time, law and order were essential to survival on the trail. In pioneer tradition we elected each other to positions of responsibility: trail boss, judge, jury members, prosecuting and defense attorneys. It was the custom of the early wagoneers to celebrate with a dance before setting out from the edge of civilization. Taking our lead from the pioneers, we chose partners for a rousing square dance on the eve of our departure.

Gordon's commanding voice early the next morning had put our wagon train in motion. As my wagon lurched forward I glanced southeast along the North Platte River. A stretch of sandy flats flecked with sagebrush ran toward the horizon but didn't quite make it. The prairie suddenly gave way to the steep flanks of Wildcat Ridge. Just in front of the ridge rose a cone-shaped mound capped with a tall spire known as Chimney Rock. The great tusk of clay and sandstone had become famous as a landmark for prairie schooners heading west.

In the mid-1800s the promise of rich farmlands in Oregon and Washington and gold strikes in California pulled tens of thousands of emigrants from the east along the Platte River. Most pioneers took the North Platte Valley route through Nebraska's panhandle. At the fork of the North and South Platte Rivers in west-central Nebraska, some wagons immediately headed along the North Platte River. Others followed the South Platte west for a short distance, then forded the river to reach the North Platte Valley. The North Platte "road" was actually a series of trails. Two became legendary: the Oregon Trail on the south bank of the North Platte, and the Mormon Trail on the north bank, which Mormon leader Brigham Young and his followers traveled in 1847 and 1848.

The North Platte Valley, which tapers nearly 200 miles across western Nebraska, began to form more than four million years before the first covered wagon appeared. The river that cuts through the broad floodplain today spreads out in shallow braided channels, except where the water backs up behind dams built for irrigation and flood control. Throughout the North Platte Valley cash crops of sugar beets, dry edible beans, corn, and alfalfa depend on irrigation from the valley's river.

"We primarily use gravity irrigation in the North Platte Valley," explained Stan Haas, an employee at Panhandle Station, a research extension service affiliated with the University of Nebraska. "At several locations along the river, farmers divert the waters of the North Platte through an extensive network of canals that run north, south, and east from the main channel. Gravity spreads the river water over the fields. Much of the excess water returns to the North Platte many miles downstream to be used again."

Farming in the North Platte Valley has changed in the last 40 years. It has progressed from the horse-drawn tillage equipment of the early days to the mammoth soil-chewing machines of today. "Despite the changes that have taken place on the land," Stan said, "the river has remained constant. It continues to dress the landscape in different shades of green, the fertility that helps people in this valley prosper."

Not far from the banks of the quiet river, our column of covered wagons bumped along State Highway 92. About noon Gordon led us off across roadless prairie. The wagons had no springs. Each jolt of the wooden wheels on the uneven grassland jarred my bones and left my backside aching. To avoid bruising punishment from the jostling and to lighten the load for the team pulling the wagon, the pioneers often walked along by the side. Our wagons jounced over hillocks at a plodding pace. When we stopped to rest, one guest said: "How disappointing it must have been in the old days to look back and almost be able to see where you had camped the night before." Indeed, 15 miles was a good day's journey in the 1800s.

During the peak years of the mid-1800s as many as 500 wagons a day rolled along the North Platte. The wagons fanned out, eight and sometimes twelve abreast, to avoid the trail dust. Where the prairie broke into ravines or bucked into steep hills, the wagons had to converge in a single column on a route that bypassed the obstacle. The iron-rimmed wheels of thousands of heavy wagons rolling over the same narrow pass gouged deep gullies in the land. One of the wagon-carved swales remains visible today at Scotts Bluff National Monument, not many miles from Nebraska's western border.

"Scotts Bluff was the first barrier of dramatic height that the pioneers encountered," Jerry Banta, superintendent of Scotts Bluff National Monument, said. "Scotts Bluff is actually an 800-foot-high promontory surrounded by smaller, rugged bluffs. These geologic formations created deep defiles that posed natural barriers to wagon trains. Gaps such as Robidoux Pass and Mitchell Pass gave the travelers a way through. Mitchell Pass lay at the center of the bluffs. The pass was so narrow and rough that each wagon had to follow the same ruts carved by the lead wagon. Consequently the wagons cut a trough eight feet deep. Today about 200,000 visitors a year come to see this imprint left by the pioneers."

By midafternoon Gordon had brought our wagon train to the end of its first day's journey. It was now twilight on the trail. Our wagons were circled around a campfire, and soon we would bed down under the stars. The glowing coals of the open fire reminded me that heat-generated forces deep inside the earth were not at rest. As in ages past, the North American continent was drifting westward at an imperceptible rate. This subtle motion has triggered earthquakes, unleashed scalding flows of lava, and raised mountainous welts of earth and stone across the face of the land. As if a balance were needed, rivers and streams long ago began carving valleys—gentle gaps of solitude. No other landform exhibits so well the calm side of nature, I thought, as I climbed into my bedroll. The night of the North Platte yawned before me, and the prairie seemed at peace.

Perky and plump, a goldfinch perches on a birch limb in the Kickapoo Valley, where fields often ring with the trills of these "wild canaries."

FOLLOWING PAGES: *Contour plowing grooms fields of grain in the Kickapoo Valley. The graceful strips protect hillside topsoil by reducing erosion.*

Labored climb up a 90-meter ramp ends in graceful downhill flight (opposite) for U. S. and
Canadian skiers competing at Westby, Wisconsin. Immigrants from Norway settled this area of
the Kickapoo Valley in the mid-1800s. Forested hills furnished timber for homes and for fuel,
and springs and creeks provided water. Today international ski-jumping contests and festivals
flavored with Norwegian dialects help maintain the valley's Nordic traditions.

80

THE WESTERN UPLANDS

Star

The grassy pastures and neatly plowed fields of Wyoming's Star Valley hurtled toward me at more than 200 feet per second. Cows grazed unperturbed a half a mile below me, while I struggled to breathe and tried to force my stomach down from my throat. Pilot Mel Barron pulled the little biplane up sharply—straight toward puffy white clouds in endless blue sky—and rolled it sideways in a complete circle. When I pried my eyes back open, we hung motionless above those same cows and fields, then pivoted backward.

"Had enough?" Mel yelled over the roar of the engine.

"Oh . . . yes," I managed to croak, envying the cows their solid ground.

"I wanted you to see what Pitts biplanes can do," Mel explained as we landed near the Pitts factory in the town of Afton. "They are the only unlimited aerobatic aircraft manufactured in the U.S."

Wyoming's Star Valley seemed an unlikely spot for an airplane factory, but I would soon discover similar surprises wrought by inventive and independent people who live in America's western uplands. This vast highland area of the United States stretches between the Rocky Mountains and the Sierra Nevada. Born of volcanic activity and the shifting of the earth's crust, the uplands cradle many valleys that lie more than 6,000 feet above sea level. In this thinly populated region—where residents must cope with dryness, rough winters, and rugged terrain—few large cities exist. For two months I explored four highland valleys and found that tomorrow can seem little changed from yesterday in pockets of the interior West.

I had arrived in western Wyoming in early spring. Snow still blanketed the Salt River Range, part of the Rockies that cup Star Valley. On the east and west the sharp summits rise nearly a mile above the flat valley floor. A fertile strip of pastures and hayfields about 10 miles wide and 40 miles long, Star Valley hugs the curves of the Salt River near the Idaho-Wyoming border. Livestock graze grasslands bordering the river; dairy farms and ranches dot a tidy checkerboard of fields. Salt Lake City, the nearest metropolitan area, lies about 200 miles south. Afton, with a population of 1,500—the valley's largest town—has been the home of Pitts Aerobatics since 1970. Outside Afton, petroleum companies drill for oil and natural gas; to the west a new phosphate mine promises industrial growth.

But for almost a century dairying has been Star's livelihood. The elevation of the valley, more than a mile above sea level, encourages early winters and shrinks the growing season to less than 60 days—barely long enough to raise hay and grain for cattle fodder. Many of the dairymen in the valley, such as Stanley Reeves, were born into the business. I joined Stan and his wife,

Wind blown mule-ears brighten a meadow on the edge of Wyoming's Star Valley. From Rocky Mountain foothills west to the Sierra Nevada, high elevation, rough terrain, and harsh weather shape the stern beauty of America's western uplands. PRECEDING PAGES: *Protected by federal law, mustangs—wild horses descended from domestic stock—run free across sagebrush on a dry Nevada flatland.*

Maggie, before six o'clock one morning in their milking shed near the community of Smoot. Stan, a gruff man in his early 50s whose dark hair is graying at the temples, herded the first 12 of his 120 cows into pens inside the building. Automatic milking machines went to work. Warm milk sloshed into calibrated glass jugs in rhythmic spurts, then flowed through a pipeline to a huge refrigerated tank. Stan is a dairyman by choice. "Dairying is the backbone of Star Valley. It's a demanding way of life. We have to milk 365 days a year, morning and night, sick or well. We live our lives in a cowshed," Stan rumbled, but his tone implied that a cowshed is the best place to be. Reeves Dairy produces more than two tons of Grade A milk daily. About 140 other farms also ship milk; most sell it to the Star Valley Cheese Cooperative in Thayne, about 15 miles north of Afton.

Signs herald the cheese factory, a faded yellow brick building dominated by white silos and flanked by the distant snowy crags of the Salt River Range. The plant opened in 1948 and soon became the major link in the valley's economy. When sewage-disposal problems closed the facility in 1982, local dairymen faced financial disaster. They reorganized the operation as a cooperative and reopened nine days later. Star Valley producers now own 50 percent of the plant; a large Utah dairy owns the other half. A thick yeasty smell permeates the factory. Workers wearing rubber boots and white paper caps sour, then gel, fresh milk in big metal vats. Others cut, cook, and stir this solution, then remove the whey. The curd—heated, stretched, then squeezed into molds—becomes Star Valley mozzarella and provolone. Each day the factory processes 420,000 pounds of milk, a job that keeps about 60 people working full time year round.

Some residents of Star Valley find seasonal jobs to supplement their incomes. From December through April, Bart Erickson, a young farmer from the town of Etna, feeds elk for the Wyoming Game and Fish Department. Thousands of these animals once wintered on native ranges in Star and other valleys. When those ranges became dairies and ranches, Wyoming began feeding the elk. Twenty-three feed grounds sustain elk herds throughout the northwestern part of the state. At Alpine Junction, Bart works on a 96-acre feeding station established near the northern edge of Star Valley in the mid-1940s. He was hitching two big, brown workhorses to a hay wagon when I met him at Alpine in late March.

Not 50 yards from us more than 600 elk watched patiently, waiting. The feed ground is fenced on only three sides, Bart explained, as we loaded the wagon; the animals know they can escape into the mountains. We climbed onto the wagon. Harnesses groaned, and the breath of the snorting horses turned white in the cold air as they pulled us through deep ruts in the muddy field. We scattered more than a hundred bales of hay as we jounced along. The elk followed us. Some still carried impressive six-point antlers, trophies that attract hunters from across the United States.

Other big game—including deer, moose, and bear—also entices hunters to the Salt River Range and to the Greys River area east of Star Valley. Along the Greys, where there are no towns and few cabins, only a couple of gas drilling rigs and campgrounds break hundreds of square miles of wilderness and national forest. The region is a hunter's paradise. Low Gardner, a native of Afton in his 60s, has been an outfitter for more than 30 years. Antlers, moose heads, and bobcat skins decorate the living-room walls of the guest

ranch that he and his wife, Ada, began in 1963—one of the first in the valley. "We never advertise, and we're still booked up by April," said Low. "Folks come from as far away as Germany and Belgium." From their windows the Gardners watch moose and deer feeding. In their creek, muskrat compete with mink, and guests can fish breakfast from a pond next to the lodge. Low loves it: "I've never found a place I'd trade this for. The mountains, the scenery, and the hunting make Star Valley special."

"And the fishing," Ada added. "Low fishes both days of summer." Summers in the valley, everyone agrees, are spectacular, but too short. "Summer is only two weeks of bad skiing, and in winter it's so cold a germ couldn't live here," Harry McReynolds, a logger and construction worker who had moved to Afton from California, told me. "But we manage to have fun."

From November through May, snowmobilers explore the high country and wooded canyons that rim the valley and edge the Greys and Little Greys Rivers. Wyoming maintains 55 miles of trails that lace this scenic backcountry. Ted Hale, who has groomed those paths for eight years for the Wyoming Recreation Commission, took me out on a frosty day in March. Blowing snow stung my cheeks as my snowmobile scooted through a blur of whiteness along the river. Snow-draped pines guarded steep slopes, and snowdrifts scalloped the Little Greys. My exhilaration increased with my speed. With Ted blazing the way, I shared more than 50 miles of the evergreen trails.

Hiking proved slower going. Bart Wilkes, who runs a sporting goods store in Afton, agreed to guide me five miles east of town to an intermittent spring, one of the few in the world. We drove two miles up Swift Creek Canyon to an impassable snowslide, then began walking. Avalanche danger is great in the steep defiles of the Salt River Range, so we had delayed our trip until late May. It was a Saturday worth waiting for.

Brilliant sunshine bounced off snowy peaks and melted drifts; reflections from Swift Creek rippled on gray rock walls. Spicy spruce scented the air, and black butterflies with golden wings flirted along the trail. High water had washed out the first bridge over the creek, so we detoured a mile up a mountainside. I began to lag behind as we climbed higher. Bart paused patiently and pointed out moose and coyote tracks, while I leaned against a twisted juniper and panted.

Tiny white and yellow wild flowers bordered the path that led us toward bridges over Swift Creek and the spring branch. Digging our fingers into wet snow, we clambered over another slide—this one about a hundred yards long and ten feet deep. Snow sometimes buries these trails into July, Bart said. Scrambling up a pile of gray scree, we found the spring—crystalline water pouring from a horizontal slit in a 6-foot-wide ledge. April through August the spring flows continuously, but Bart has seen it stop many times. "The flow slows," he said, "then stops completely and the bed dries. It starts again with a roar. Indians called the stream 'Spring that Breathes' and came here to bathe away their ills."

All Afton residents rely on the spring today. The town's entire water supply is gravity fed through a pipeline buried in the mouth of the spring.

FOLLOWING PAGES: *In a Christmas-card setting, draft horses pull a sleigh past quaking aspen. Royce Hoopes and his family will scatter the bales of hay across the new-fallen snow for dairy cattle at their Star Valley farm.*

After a long, refreshing drink of the cold water we returned to town. Along the way Bart pointed out many houses that belong to his relatives. "My great-grandfather was one of the early settlers here," he said. "A lot of people have to leave the valley to find work. All you can do here really is ranch, work in the oil fields, or have your own business."

Cattleman King Cranney ranched in Star Valley for half a century. Retired now, he is a large man in his 70s with a fringe of white hair and gray eyebrows curling toward astonishingly blue eyes. His stories reach back to 1880, when his grandfather homesteaded in Star Valley. He recalls, at age 8, riding his little mare to tell neighbors they had calls on the only phone in town—his father's. His mother told him of dancing with outlaw Butch Cassidy, who twice wintered nearby. King's grandfather, one of the first medical doctors in Star Valley, was a Mormon who had three wives. Like most of the valley's pioneers he had come to this isolated spot to escape prosecution for polygamy.

Brigham Young, head of the Church of Jesus Christ of Latter-day Saints, encouraged Mormon colonization in the West. He had heard of Star Valley and sent a party to examine it. Written accounts report that Moses Thatcher, leader of that group, declared it "the Star of All Valleys." Although trappers and mountain men—Jim Bridger, Kit Carson, Bill Sublette—had traversed the wilds surrounding Star in the 1830s and although the Lander Cutoff—a spur of the Oregon Trail—had carried thousands of pioneers through the valley, few people settled. Star Valley began attracting Mormons in the early 1880s. Public outcry against a Mormon man having more than one wife at the same time led to the Anti-Polygamy Act of 1882. Mormons found a haven in Star Valley. Today it remains a Mormon stronghold; eight out of ten residents belong to the Mormon church.

Salt Lake

Even before they settled Star Valley, the Mormons had sought refuge. In 1846 a small group led by Brigham Young fled religious persecution in Illinois. They migrated west more than 1,320 miles to the basin of the Great Salt Lake in northern Utah. When they arrived, the valley was an arid oblong of sagebrush and sand, rimmed by the jagged Wasatch Range on the east and the Oquirrh Mountains on the west. The briny shallows of an immense lake formed the northwestern boundary. Within a few days Brigham Young had laid out the two-mile-square "City of the Great Salt Lake." Workers diverted mountain streams to irrigate the desert and began creating the capital of the Mormon world.

Today a metropolitan oasis glittering across 764 square miles, Salt Lake City and its suburbs serve as home to four out of ten Utahns. East of town a large monument commemorates the arrival of the first Mormons who entered the valley in 1847. Salt Lake City exalts its Mormon heritage. Temple Square, the spiritual heart of the church of Latter-day Saints and originally the geographical center of the city, covers ten acres. As I entered the courtyard of the square, pansies blooming in a melting snowbank caught my eye. Yellow crocuses and red tulips nodded at the base of a tree. Looming with solemn authority, the granite bastion of the Mormon Temple lifts six graceful spires, the tallest crowned by a golden angel. Workers labored 40 years to complete the temple. It has been closed to all but devout Mormons since 1893, but the oval tabernacle nearby welcomes visitors of all faiths.

Awed by the tabernacle's great domed roof, I stepped inside the sanctuary and slipped quietly into a pew. The building, which seats more than 6,000 people, envelops its visitors in near acoustical perfection. A sound as slight as a straight pin hitting the wooden floor can be heard clearly throughout the sanctuary. The joy of attending Sunday services or hearing a musical performance in the building draws people from many parts of the world. I settled back for a morning concert and welcomed the soaring voices of the world-famous Mormon Tabernacle Choir.

Mormon sites and songs and the recreational appeal of the area have made tourism one of the largest industries in Salt Lake Valley. More than 130,000 tourists come annually to sample what Utahns call "the Greatest Snow on Earth." Within an hour's drive of Salt Lake City, mountain slopes and dry powder at seven resorts promise five months of superb winter skiing.

Evening snow clouds moved in, and Salt Lake City twinkled below me as I drove along the Wasatch to Little Cottonwood Canyon, where Snowbird Ski Resort nestles. Modern high rises blend into the rocky Wasatch scenery at Snowbird. The complex includes lodges, shops offering everything from gourmet cookware to custom tailoring, and restaurants serving selections from tacos to filet mignon. Skiers, I saw, do not stop when the lifts do. The electronic game room beeped and squawked, and the dance floors throbbed with festive mobs late into the night.

Snow curtained trails and trees the next morning. I struggled into my heavy boots and clomped up to a ski class. I was assigned to Jo Ann Field, a petite brunette with a warm smile. "Put your weight on your left leg to turn right," Jo Ann said. "Come up, then sink down on your right leg to turn left." Like an awkward duckling I followed her down a trail, trying to copy her movements. "Up, down, up, down," she chanted. Suddenly, I sank. My skis hit a patch of powder, vanished out of sight, and I plunged into dry fluff, kicking up a white cloud. Jo Ann laughed with me as I struggled upright. "You have to keep your weight more equal when skiing powder," she said. "Once you've mastered it, there's nothing better. It's like floating."

Late in the afternoon I tried floating the steep trails alone. Snow fell faster, veiling giant evergreens and pointed Wasatch peaks. Even with goggles, I could see no farther than 50 yards. But no matter. The mountain was mine; it enchanted and encouraged me. I had wings. Euphoric, I glided in silence, swooping past fir and spruce. That evening I found an easy chair by a cheery fireplace in a lodge and watched fat snowflakes drift past a wall of windows. Beyond them, dark figures strolled pathways hemmed with trees. Inside, counterpoint to laughter and conversations, country music drifted from hidden speakers. Fatigue washed over me—a pleasant weariness. Contented and warm, I finally understood why people buckle on clumsy boots, strap on unwieldy skis, and spend hours on a cold mountain.

Record snow made skiing great throughout the Wasatch in 1983, but the price was high. The heaviest snowmelt in Utah's history triggered spring mud slides and flooding that destroyed property worth millions of dollars. To divert high stream water, Salt Lake City residents sandbagged several streets and turned them into runoff canals; the governor declared one-third of the state's 29 counties disaster areas. Wet weather hurt industries, too. At Saltair, the Morton salt factory near the Great Salt Lake, rain caused flooding that ruined nearly 60,000 tons of salt, about one-third of the annual crop. Ray Christensen has worked at Saltair for 35 years. "We harvest in fall and spring," he told me. "This is the first time rain has flooded us out since I've been here." Morton pumps water from the Great Lake to shallow ponds, where sun rays evaporate the water and concentrate the salt. This saline solution crystallizes in smaller garden ponds. "Our harvesting machine peels off the salt layer like someone peeling an orange," Ray explained.

The Great Salt Lake contains about eight billion tons of salt. The briny expanse, some 80 miles long and 40 miles wide, is all that remains of prehistoric, freshwater Lake Bonneville. Thousands of years ago this inland sea covered 19,000 square miles in much of present-day Utah and portions of southern Idaho and eastern Nevada. Rain and feeder streams washing down from the mountains leached salt and other minerals from rocks and carried the deposits into the lake. Approximately 15,000 years ago climatic changes spawned a warming spell. Droughtlike temperatures and evaporation caused the water level of Bonneville to drop, leaving behind great concentrations of mineral salts in a lake bed more than a million years old.

Jordan

Northwest of the Great Salt Lake basin, sagebrush and tumbleweed dot thousands of square miles of mountain and desert. Crossing into the southeastern corner of Oregon, I found the rural isolation of Jordan Valley a sharp contrast to the urban valley of the Great Salt Lake. This is desolate country—a semiarid region nearly a mile high, where less than 15 inches of rain fall each year. Space and distance are overwhelming here. Brown buttes flecked with gnarled junipers overlook sloping plains of sage and grass. Green splotches of irrigated pastureland and stands of willows line Jordan Creek. The stream rises in the Owyhee Mountains and flows 50 miles west to the Owyhee River. Michael Jordan, for whom the valley is named, led a prospecting party that struck gold near the headwaters of the stream in 1863. Soon after, miners and homesteaders began moving into the mountains and canyon areas of eastern Oregon and western Idaho.

One of the first settlers in Jordan Valley was Silas Skinner, a sailor from the Isle of Man who had jumped ship in San Francisco. Silas settled on prime land on the north side of Jordan Creek near the town of Jordan Valley. As the town developed into an important stopover for miners and freighters, Silas built and ran a toll road from the mines. Later he turned to the job of raising trotting horses. His descendants today own and operate one of the largest cattle operations in the valley.

"The West was wide-open range in my great-grandfather's day," said Bob Skinner, Sr., a soft-spoken man in his early 60s. In the late 1800s federal acts offering 160 acres stimulated the flow of settlers to the valley, Mr. Skinner explained. But the policies for using the land were lax, and overgrazing by large herds damaged productive grasslands. Livestock industry leaders, fearing that too many animals were ruining the grazing, lobbied for regulations that would preserve the range. In 1934 Congress passed the Taylor Grazing Act, which controlled grazing on federal lands. Today the Bureau of Land Management (BLM), a branch of the U. S. Department of Interior, determines how many animals may feed on public lands. About half of the 1,100 people who live in the Jordan Valley area raise cattle and lease a large portion of their grazing from the BLM.

Mr. Skinner's son, Bob, is a younger edition of his tall and lanky father. "The romantic image some people have of ranchers just isn't so," Bob said. "It's true we're independent. We have to be so we can cope out here. There's a lot that goes into running a ranch—more than you can find in books. It's a long-term learning process." Bob earned his degree in business from the College of Idaho and is a licensed pilot. But his knowledge reaches far beyond the classroom. He pointed to a field on our left. "That," he said, "has not been treated or seeded and was overgrazed. See how much big sage and rabbitbrush there is. That one," he said, indicating an area of high grass, "is a perfect example of what the natural range would look like. But that's not the best grass either. It's too old and coarse, not appealing to cattle. Grass needs to be grazed, but not overgrazed, to be kept tender and productive."

Jordan Valley was part of the Vale Project, a pilot program to rehabilitate the western range. Extensive seeding, reservoirs, and livestock water systems have restored the overgrazed rangelands in the valley. At one of the seedings Bob showed me acres of crested wheat—a hardy and fast-growing plant sown in overgrazed areas. "For someone used to trees, the high desert might be boring," he said. "But I see variety every minute."

In his Cessna, Bob flew me over the valley. Below us purple lupine bloomed between silvery green clumps of sage. Pheasants and long-billed curlews darted toward willows and thickets of wild roses along Jordan Creek. A checkerboard of pale green seedings and grayer green plots of native range ended abruptly at the Jordan Craters, a 30-square-mile field of fresh basalt cinder cones and lava flows north of Jordan Creek. We circled over a huge gray crater surrounded by reddish cinders; a few sagebrush clung inside the deep cavity. These lava flows, about 9,000 years old, are among the youngest in the continental U. S. The gray-black surface, cracked and crinkled like cooked brownies, looks barren. Ripples, boils, and bubbles of lava are frozen in hard and crunchy basalt. Beyond the craters the Owyhee River has carved a deep gorge through lava and ash. Dark and light layers alternate in sheer walls that reach as high as a thousand feet.

Early evening light muted miles of grass and sagebrush as I drove toward the Cliffs of Rome, weathered rock walls near the confluence of Jordan Creek and the Owyhee. Free-form clouds hung in a pink sky, quilting fields with their shadows. It was nearly sunset when I reached the cliffs, where a thick basalt layer caps beige volcanic ash and sedimentary layers of an ancient riverbed. The curved buttes reminded settlers, who named them, of ancient Roman ruins. At my approach cliff swallows chattered and fussed about their nests. Young quail, their curved crests bobbing like ladies' fancy hats, scurried to refuge in tall grass lining the road. I glimpsed four mule deer winding slowly across a rock face 150 feet above the water. Carved and worn by erosion, the cliffs stand like pale medieval castles. A   (Continued on page 104)

Churning muddy slush, chariots tear along a quarter-mile track in Afton. The people of Star Valley have relished winter racing for more than half a century; in dry snow they compete in light sleds called cutters.

FOLLOWING PAGES: *Wild henbane blooms in early July as a mare, with her three-day-old foal, nibbles new grass. Spring comes late in Star Valley because of long winters. Beyond the corral and the weathered barn, pockets of snow persist on the slopes of the Salt River Range.*

"*The Greatest Snow on Earth.*" *Dry, light powder in Utah froths knee-high as a skier hurtles down a challenging trail at Snowbird. This ski resort above Salt Lake Valley casts a welcome glow in the frosty dusk of the Wasatch Mountains (right). Snowbird records an average snowfall of 450 inches a year. Taillights trace the winding road through Little Cottonwood Canyon. In the distance glitters Salt Lake City.*

I nspired voices of the Mormon Tabernacle Choir blend in harmony during a Sunday concert in Salt

Lake City's Tabernacle—a building noted for its near-perfect acoustics. Mormon leader Brigham Young founded the chorus in 1847; it now numbers some 350 members. All the singers, like alto Mary Stewart Hunsaker (opposite), volunteer their talents.

Agile in flight but awkward on land, American white pelicans soar above wetlands east of Utah's Great Salt Lake. Despite its arid basin-and-range *landscape, Utah has one of the largest waterfowl breeding grounds in the nation. Thousands of pelicans nest each summer in the freshwater marshes that surround the salty lake.*

golden eagle perched on one turret; silhouetted against the darkening sky, its mate soared toward the Owyhee.

The next day I headed back toward the river to join rancher Jim Matteri as he turned his cattle out to spring pasture. Jim, driving a pickup truck, led a parade up U.S. 95. Behind him on horseback, neighboring rancher Richard Madariaga and several ranch hands drove 253 head of Herefords and black bally single file down a steep bend toward the water. Driving a van to protect the animals from traffic, I followed. Just beyond the bridge over the Owyhee we started trailing the cattle overland. I parked the van and flung myself onto Tracy, my horse for the day.

Gray clouds dripped rain, and the wind picked up. Richard's teenage daughter Sheila—her blond braids flapping—galloped beside the herd, yipping and slapping her reins to keep the cows in line. I forced my heels down and gripped Tracy's flanks with my knees as she shambled through big clumps of sage. By late afternoon we had driven the cows 11 miles to our destination—a metal gate in a sea of crested wheat. In the fenced BLM seeding beyond the gate the cattle would graze for about two months, then the herd would move on to another federal pasture.

From Jim Matteri and Richard Madariaga I sensed that ranching is a way of life for the whole family, not just an occupation. Ranchers Ralph and Kay Fillmore strengthened that understanding. When I arrived at their corral, Kay had just helped deliver a calf. Her eldest son, Mark, 16, struggled to carry the wet and shivering newborn to the barn. "Calves, like babies," Kay said, "arrive any time, day or night."

Heifers, cows birthing for the first time, often need help. In the darkness of a cowshed I held my breath while Ralph pulled a calf from a heifer. Clint, the Fillmores' youngest son, assisted. Hooking chains to the calf's head and feet, Ralph began to tug gently. Ever so slowly Ralph eased the calf from its mother. The newborn lay unmoving on the straw. Ralph quickly cleared membrane from its nose, then gently tickled its nostrils with a blade of straw until the calf cried and struggled weakly. That task completed, Ralph hurried to doctor a sick cow, then spent nearly half an hour trying to teach an abandoned calf to nurse from a bottle. Each of Ralph's movements reflected patience, respect, and affection for the animals.

Judi and Mike Hanley, like the other ranchers I met in Jordan Valley, showed that same care and commitment. Judi drove me out on their horse-drawn hay wagon to feed cattle south of Jordan Creek. Among willows near the water, new calves wobbled at their mothers' sides. Some, a few weeks older, scampered away, kicking their back legs straight out and twisting their tails as if they had springs in their backs. Two sandhill cranes stopped eating as we neared and called to each other, their *gar-oo-oo* cries resembling the sound of a broken gate swinging on rusty hinges. Back at the ranch house, I visited with Mike, a fourth generation Oregonian. He proudly showed me a 120-year-old stagecoach and other polished carriages that he has restored. Similar rigs had brought settlers to Jordan Valley. In basic ways the valley remains unchanged from pioneer days. "Our growing season is short; water is limited," Mike said. "We do what we can here—like our fathers did before us. We ranch. There's nothing much here to argue over. We've just got one thing—cows."

Before the Taylor Grazing Act imposed range restrictions, Jordan Valley was sheep country too. Many of the sheepmen were Basques from the western Pyrenees, mountains of northern Spain and southern France. Basques, who have their own language and represent one of the oldest cultures in western Europe, were drawn to the U.S. during the California gold rush. Some of the immigrants who worked in the nearby Idaho mines about 1885 later established ranches and businesses in Jordan Valley. "My dad came here from Spain in 1900," Fred Eiguren, a Basque cattleman, told me. "There were thousands of sheep then. The Great Depression ruined a lot of people. The Taylor Grazing Act was the final blow. You had to own land to get grazing; many sheepmen didn't, and cattlemen ruled the range. There's no better cow country than Jordan Valley. Everyone knows everybody for a hundred miles, and your neighbor is there to help when you need him."

Branding is a major event marked on the cattleman's calendar. Fred and his sons work much like wranglers of the Old West. One horseman drops a rope over a calf's head; the other throws a loop around its hind legs. While the calf lies stretched on its back between two horses, another ranch hand brands it. Other hands notch the ears, then dehorn and castrate the animal. In less than a minute the calf scrambles up and lopes off shaking its head.

Cows bawled everywhere. The smell of singed hair hung heavy in smoky air. Branding irons heated in a propane flame. Tim Lequerica, a grizzle-bearded Basque, put a hand on my arm. "Ready to try?" he asked. I nodded. "Kneel on the calf so it can't move," Tim said, "then stamp the brand solidly into the hide. Hold on because the iron tends to slide. When you're done, the mark should be the color of bread crust."

I swallowed hard, took hold of the long-handled iron, and approached a two-month-old calf. Holding it down, I found, was a lot harder than it looked; calves that age weigh about 250 pounds—most of it muscle. I jammed the iron onto the animal's side and clung desperately to the handle. A cloud of white smoke and a burning stench rose. Nervously I glanced up at Tim. He nodded. "You've got it. Hold on." Muscles quivered along the calf's side, and it bleated plaintively. My muscles cramped from tension and strain. Long seconds later, I lifted the brand to find the toasty outline of an oarlock.

"See," said Tim. "Easy."

I knew differently.

Ranchers take a break from their chores for two days in May to attend Jordan Valley's biggest celebration—the annual rodeo. The event affords modern-day wranglers a chance to display traditional cowboy skills honed on the range. The whole valley turns out for the rodeo, and hundreds of spectators come from miles beyond the region to pack the bleachers north of town.

From his opening words—"It's *rodeo* time in Jordan Valley"—veteran announcer Dick Parker, his brown cowboy hat tipped over curly gray hair and blue eyes, entertained us. "Ride that horse!" he urged a young man who had a death grip on a mean black bucking mount. Kicking hard, one particularly energetic bronc flipped a rider high into the air. The flying contestant landed with a bone-bruising thud. "A spectacular dismount," Dick observed. "Give him a big hand, folks, cause that's all this cowboy's gonna get."

The crowd grew quiet when Dick called the main event—The Big Loop—in which two buckaroos each use 20-foot loops to rope a running horse. Each competitor on the team must handle at least 50 feet of rope, and each must control the twirling loop as he gallops to lasso the moving horse. One cowboy ropes the horse's head; his partner then catches the animal's front feet. The cowhands must stop the horse without tripping it. The job looked impossible, yet the winning team did it in a little over 16 seconds.

At the rodeo's close, friends lingered, enjoying one of the few chances to socialize in a land where distances are great and people are few.

Steptoe

South of Jordan Valley, in Nevada, the population density is also sparse—fewer than eight persons per square mile. Silver and gold strikes in the late 1800s lured settlers to the territory. Some of the prospectors struck it rich in Steptoe, a valley that basks high and dry more than 6,000 feet above sea level. Steptoe lies in eastern Nevada and measures 15 miles wide and about 100 miles long. This narrow strip of sagebrush and scrub gives way to piñon pine and juniper that sprinkle the craggy mountains of the Egan Range on the west and the Schell Creek Range on the east.

At Schellbourne in the foothills of the Schell Creek Range, sheep and cattle graze the former domain of Indians, stagecoaches, and Pony Express riders. Shoshone and Paiute lived here originally. In the mid-1800s the Butterfield Overland Mail established a station; an Army garrison at Schellbourne protected gold seekers rushing west. In 1860—when the Pony Express began service from St. Joseph, Missouri, to Sacramento, California—Schellbourne served as a relay stop. Today the ruins of a stone warehouse front a tree-lined path winding down from the mountains. It's easy to imagine a buckskin-clad courier galloping beneath the branches—a boy who would dare to answer an ad seeking "young, skinny, wiry fellows not over eighteen. Must be expert riders, willing to risk death daily. Orphans preferred." One of those "expert riders" was Richard Erastus Egan from Steptoe Valley. The Egan Range took its name from his father, Howard Egan.

When gold and silver production waned in the late 1800s, copper revived Steptoe. In 1907 Nevada Consolidated Copper Company completed a railroad through the middle of the valley and began hauling ore north from vast deposits near Ely, the county seat and the valley's largest town. In 1933 Kennecott Copper Corporation took over the mines and the railway. For more than 70 years the open-pit mine at Ruth, one of the largest in the world, was the major employer in the valley. When copper prices fell in 1978, the mine closed; the Kennecott smelter in McGill shut down in 1983.

Passing the smelter's idle smokestacks, A. Z. Joy and I drove north from Ely. A boisterous man in his early 50s, A. Z. has been the county agricultural extension agent in Steptoe for 24 years. The road ran straight to the horizon. Miles of sagebrush punctuated by an occasional tree unrolled before us. "Everywhere you see trees," A. Z. boomed, "there is either a spring or a ranch. The trees have been planted. This is ranching country. Steptoe is fine grazing, but it's very dry. In summertime even the jackrabbits carry canteens."

Clouds cast gray shadows on the sage, and the gauzy white sheet of a spring storm indicated a distant shower. "Mustangs." A. Z. pointed. "Over there." A chestnut stallion, its harem of seven mares, and two colts eyed us from open range near the road. Fifty years ago so many wild horses roamed the valley that ranchers rounded up thousands and shipped them off for sale. Many ranchers resent the animals because they compete with livestock for forage. Federal law has protected the horses since 1971, and their numbers are increasing.

A white wave—a band of 2,000 sheep—curled across the road ahead. "Ewes," A. Z. told me. "They're on their way to shearing and lambing grounds." Like Jordan Valley, Steptoe once sheltered thousands of sheep. Falling wool and lamb prices hurt the industry. Today only four sheep companies remain in the area. John Uhalde & Company, founded by a Basque sheepherder at the turn of the century, is one of the oldest. Gracian Uhalde and his wife, Rena, manage the sheep now.

Snow still draped the Egan Range when I met the Uhaldes at their shearing camp in Jakes Valley west of Ely. Gracian is in his early 30s with light brown hair and a drooping mustache bleached by the sun. Rena, tall and graceful, has short dark hair. "My grandfather came from France at the turn of the century and herded sheep in Idaho," Gracian told me as we sat and drank coffee in an old yellow school bus that serves as camp kitchen and dining room. "He started the ranch near here almost 75 years ago. In the late '30s we bought winter range about 110 miles south. We've got about 5,000 head of sheep and trail them back and forth. We shear here every spring. In June we herd a band across Steptoe to summer near Berry Creek. We get two crops from sheep: wool and meat. Timing shearing is tricky; it should happen after the cold and snow that can kill newly shorn animals, but before lambing."

An itinerant shearing team meets the needs of the sheepmen in Steptoe. The shearers were due the next day. Before they arrived, Gracian wanted to separate the early lambers, which would be sheared first, from the late lambers. Whooping and hollering, Gracian and two herders forced the ewes through a narrow wooden run. Gracian manipulated a movable gate in the enclosure, driving early lambers into a corral. Rena counted the late lambers as they rocketed out of the chute. I tried to work the gate, but the animals were too big, too strong, and too fast for me. One tried to leap the gate. I grabbed its curly fleece and almost went flying out of the chute.

Shearing, I found the next day, was no easier. I crawled out of bed at 3:30 a.m. and arrived at the Uhaldes in time to watch the shearing crew roll in. The men pitched a long canvas tent in the cold sunshine and fired up a portable generator. Whirring electric clippers and the bleating of hundreds of sheep drowned the liquid conversation of the Spanish-speaking crew. Each man grabbed a ewe from a holding pen in front of the tent, dragged it to his clippers, knelt on the animal, tied its legs with a rawhide thong, and removed its fleece—all in about three minutes.

The task looked deceptively easy. I wanted to try it. The heavy clippers, snarling and rotating in my hand, had a mind of their own. Sharp blades lunged toward my fingers. Thick wool fought every effort to slice through it. It took me several ragged swipes to reach the animal's hide. Twenty minutes later, half finished, and totally worn out, I gratefully passed on the job. By late afternoon more than a thousand fleeces were packed into long burlap bags for sale and shipment. Ewes nicked by the clippers needed to be treated against infection. Gracian handed me a long pole with a tiny crook at the end. Wielding it, I snagged shorn sheep by the legs, pulled them toward me, wrestled them to the ground, then struggled to hold them while Gracian sprayed antiseptic on their cuts.

After dusk we gathered for dinner in the bus. My muscles ached from wrestling sheep. I slumped onto a bench between Rena and Gracian. "Sheepmen are an endangered species," Gracian said as we ate. "No one really wants to work like this under these conditions any more. It's too tough. Coyotes are one of our biggest problems. Their numbers have increased since the government outlawed the use of poison on federal lands in 1972. Coyotes kill hundreds of our lambs."

The skeptical humor of a bumper sticker that I saw—"Eat Nevada Lamb. 10,000 Coyotes Can't Be Wrong"—doesn't dismay men like Mel Anderson. Mel supervises predation control for the U.S. Fish and Wildlife Service. On horseback and in helicopters he scours the range for coyotes. We mounted horses at the Uhalde lambing grounds and picked our way upward among tall piñon pines. Mel scanned the dry ground as we rode. "You can learn a lot about coyotes by their tracks," he said, "where they're denning, how many there are. It takes a little lookin' and a little ridin', but after two or three days, you've got a good idea of what's going on. See," he said, pointing to a big paw print, "probably a male, headed into the valley."

Plundering by coyotes has persuaded most ranchers in Steptoe to switch from sheep to cattle. In this tough country many cattlemen must run hundreds of head to make a profit. But some small operators, mostly old-timers whose mortgages are paid, survive in Steptoe. Joe Salvi, born in the valley, is in his 70s now, white haired and stooped, with bushy eyebrows and a weathered face. Joe makes ends meet with about a hundred head of cattle. When I arrived at his ranch near Cherry Creek, he was painstakingly planting corn, kernel by kernel. He stopped and asked me into his home. Pipes funnel water from a nearby hot spring to warm his house, and he swims nearly every day of the year in a century-old pool fed and heated by the same spring. At my request Joe folded himself into a chair, his small dog at his knee, and played the accordion. "Don't know any of that modern jitterbug," he said,"only old songs." He played nostalgic ballads from his youth, and he played them well, his callused fingers deftly rippling the keys.

Change may come slowly to some of these valleys, I thought as I sat at Ely's airport, waiting for the plane that would take me from the western uplands. The region's rigors of dry and cold weather, rugged terrain, and high elevation forge tenacious and independent individuals who cherish their pasts, their futures, and their friends. Suddenly a touch on my arm broke my reverie. I looked up into the faces of Rena, Gracian, and their four children. They had driven nearly two hours from their sheep ranch to say good-bye and to give me a special memento—a luxurious white sheepskin.

As my plane climbed above the valley—no aerobatics this time—Steptoe disappeared beneath a fluffy cloud layer. I leaned back in my seat, twined my fingers in the curly fleece, and rested my chin in its softness. In the Uhaldes and others like them I had discovered the essence of those upland valleys—not the topography but the people.

At home on the range, wrangler Bill Whitfield grips a rawhide romal—a flexible whip attached to the reins of his horse. After a short break he will return to branding Herefords, a spring chore in Oregon's Jordan Valley.

For a bone-jarring eight seconds, a contestant rides out the fury of a bucking bull in the annual Jordan Valley Rodeo. If a rider falls, the clowns tackle the serious challenge of distracting the bull so the cowboy can escape the threat of a mauling.

FOLLOWING PAGES: *Buttes of basalt and volcanic ash, the Cliffs of Rome face a moonlit road on the bank of the Owyhee River near Jordan Valley. Each spring, hundreds of boaters float this stretch of the river, part of Oregon's scenic waterway system.*

KERBY SMITH

Higﬂ-speed haircuts: It takes only three minutes for a skilled shearer using electric clippers to peel off a sheep's thick fleece. This shearing team crops about 5,000 sheep every spring in the Steptoe Valley region of Nevada. A shorn ewe that lost its lamb suckles an orphan (far left). To encourage the mother to adopt the infant, herders dressed it in the hide of the ewe's stillborn baby. Left: In a few days this new lamb will grow to fit into its own baggy skin.

115

S*agebrush reclaims the right-of-way in Currie and chokes the wheels of an idled freight wagon (opposite) on a nearby ranch. During the early 1900s the now-abandoned warehouse and train station in Steptoe Valley served as a busy shipping point for sheep and cattle. The Nevada Northern locomotives that stopped here also carried shipments of copper mined from an open-pit 75 miles southwest of Currie. Today such deserted buildings and silent crossroads in Steptoe evoke the rigors of survival in the valleys of America's western uplands.*

Plateaus and Basins of

Verde

Transfixed, I watched the drama of nature around me. I saw illusions unfold. A fan of mist opened to conceal the face of a hill. A dark thunderbird of a storm, beating outstretched wings in warning, trailed shadowy plumes of rain across the valley. And a rainbow gestured a prism arc to touch a mesa.

That theater of natural wonder, Arizona's Verde Valley, is one of many dramatic valleys in an area that extends from the southwestern United States across the border into the southern part of Mexico. Millions of years ago churning geologic forces uplifted this region and turned it into a land of basins, ranges, and plateaus. In this varied expanse I would visit four valleys: each landscape different, each both a haven and a place of conflict, and each a shaper of human lives and stories.

The first Anglo-American settlers in the Verde Valley had come in search of a richer life. Much of the Southwest was newly American; it had been formed from the northern part of Mexico, which that country had ceded to the United States in 1848. In the territory that would later become Arizona, land awaited new owners. Pioneers crossed great distances to stake out farms in the Verde, located between the present towns of Flagstaff and Prescott. From sheer cliffs of the Mogollon Rim along the northeastern edge of the valley and from the formidable Black Hills along the southwestern edge, settlers gazed down upon an oasis. The sheltered land that lay before them was shaded by cottonwood trees and laced with streams. By tradition it was the home of the Yavapai and Apache Indians, but soldiers stationed at a bastion near the center of the valley guarded it as settlers' land. One new arrival saw it immediately as "a hunter's and stockman's paradise. Wild game was everywhere and the grass was knee high and plentiful."

This sanctuary, however, afforded no easy passage. Already exhausted from months of travel, often sick, constantly in fear of Indian attack, most Verde settlers faced one last obstacle before they could enter the valley. They had to struggle down a steep promontory named Grief Hill. One young pioneer in his later years recalled such a harrowing descent: "Regardless of our having a wagon with good brakes, strong horses with good harness, Stepdad had to cut a tree and tie it on behind [the wagon]; yet, so steep was that road that even then the wagon crowded the horses. I recall [him] telling Mother he would be damned if he would ever drive that road again. He didn't." People stayed and put down roots. Many of the pioneers settled along Oak Creek where they had found "all that good water and land that would raise anything from cabbages to roses, from fish to Herefords."

These Anglo-American settlers were latecomers in the human drama of

Oak Creek mirrors spires of Cathedral Rock in Arizona's Verde Valley region.
From southern Mexico into the Southwest, valleys share a geologic past of
upheaval and a heritage of Indian settlement and Spanish conquest.
PRECEDING PAGES: *In the Verde Valley a limestone cliff shelters five-story*
Montezuma Castle, one of the nation's best preserved cliff dwellings.

the Verde Valley. By 10,000 years ago bands of Indians roamed this region in search of wild plants and game; by A.D. 700, farmers tilled irrigated fields and traded copper and salt from the Verde's mines. Population increased, and villages grew. About A.D. 1100, other groups migrated into the Verde from high on the Mogollon Rim, or perhaps from the desert to the south. Cliff dwellings and fortresslike pueblos became common. Gradually, whole populations crowded into larger but fewer communal dwellings. Finally, about 1400, the inhabitants began to leave the valley. Whether drought, overcrowding, disease, or a combination of misfortunes drove them away remains uncertain. The scraps of living they left behind are poignant testimony: pieces of intricately woven cloth, fiber sandals, shell jewelry adorned with turquoise, pottery painted in geometric designs, the remains of cooking fires, bits of food. The ruins and artifacts of these prehistoric valley people remain awesome touchstones of the past.

On an April morning I first saw one of the famous ruins, Montezuma Well. Jack Beckman, a National Park Service Ranger, met me at the huge pit. Its mouth measures 470 feet in diameter, and its sheer edge drops 70 feet to the water surface. "I love this place," Jack said. "Come, I'll show it to you." He led me down into the limestone sink, past abandoned cliff dwellings, down to where horned pondweed and miner's lettuce grow within the well's shallows and wild currants and Arizona walnuts thrive along its banks.

"Fish cannot live here," Jack said. "Some people say they do. That's a lot of pickle smoke. Too much carbon dioxide in the water." Red-winged blackbirds, however, seemed to flourish in the bracing air. They perched in the trees and sang cheerfully. Nearby, a tiny black phoebe tended a pocket-shaped nest attached to the wall of a rock shelter that Indians had occupied. A rust-colored rock squirrel nibbling hackberry buds stopped and gave us a solemn stare. "Hello, squirrel," Jack said. The animals seemed to know that he would not bother them. Nor does he disturb the feathered prayer sticks that Indian visitors often leave near the well. He knows this is a holy place. We left the interior part of the pit and strolled down the well's rocky outer face. We stopped where water was flowing up through a deep rift and into a stone-lined channel. "Navajo, Hopi, and Yavapai come here for this water. I have watched them dip it up and take it away. It's sacred," Jack said.

The waters of Montezuma Well mean life itself to the Tonto Apaches. One of the Apaches who grew up in the Verde met me at Tuzigoot, a stone ruin of a pueblo built high on a bluff and abandoned at about the same time as the village at the well. Wanda Padilla, a National Park Service Ranger, spoke of her people and the role of the well.

"My grandmother was more than a hundred years old when she died in 1969. She cooked in a wickiup beside the Verde River and spoke only Apache. She told me our creation myth when I was a child." Wanda's dark eyes softened: "Montezuma Well flooded the world, and there was only one person left, a girl, Widapokwi. She floated in a canoe until it came to rest near a red-rock cave. That's where she lived. Beneath it grew an oak grove, and she lived on the acorns. The lady bore a daughter whose father was the sun. The daughter produced a son; this was the start of the people.

"My father took us to those oak groves near Boynton Pass where our people began," Wanda added softly. "When I am feeling low, or depressed, I can visit red-rock country, where the myth started, and feel much better.

"My great-grandfather was the principal chief of the Oak Creek Apaches. He was called Ndé Ndé-z, Tall Man. He camped mostly in the area of the present town of Sedona and south of it along the red sandstone bluffs. Members of other bands sometimes referred to the whole Oak Creek band as 'The People of Ndé Ndé-z.' His son, my grandfather, was an Apache medicine man—and an army scout at Fort Verde. His Indian name was What rè Sama, hard for the soldiers to pronounce or spell, so they named him Henry Ward Beecher. He died before I was born. They dressed him in his army uniform and placed his medicine bag with him. My grandmother opened it before they buried him. She had always wanted to know its secrets. There were many things inside, including a clear crystal stone. That stone was his power."

The sacred power of Henry Ward Beecher was a legacy of long religious tradition among North American Indians. The Tuzigoot museum displays such a jewel-faceted quartz crystal among other artifacts archaeologists have discovered in the area. Nearly half of the excavated burials were skeletons of children eight years old or younger—evidence of how fragile survival was in this corner of the valley. Perhaps it was decreasing food sources that had made relocation necessary for the prehistoric Indians of Tuzigoot.

I drove into red-rock country northeast of the valley, to the sandstone bluffs near Sedona and to the raw terrain near Boynton Pass. Eroded over time by wind and water into shapes that range in color from vibrant reds to beige, the land looks like the exposed blood and bones of the earth. Viewing this landscape is like witnessing creation itself. The first outsiders to enter the valley area were five Spaniards led by explorer Antonio de Espejo. Seeking gold and silver mines, his expedition followed Hopi guides into the Verde in May of 1583. The party encountered a group of Indians, the Yavapai. "All the men, women, and children were seated in a row, with their heads low, singing of the peace they wished with us," wrote one of the Spaniards. "Many of them accompanied us to the mines . . . so worthless that we did not find in any of them a trace of silver, as they were copper mines, and poor."

The explorers had searched the area near the present site of Jerome. Four centuries later to the month, I visited the town. It slumps against Cleopatra Hill, a mountain once rich in copper, along with some gold and silver. After miners staked a claim here in the 1870s, there was nowhere to go but rich.

By 1929 Jerome had boomed to become Arizona's third largest town. Some 2,400 miners worked vast open-pits and 88 miles of dark shafts and tunnels. In 1953 mining stopped after 77 years, and many people left the shaky town. Long before, weakened from tunneling, dynamite blasts, and mud slides, Cleopatra Hill began to shift and shudder. Jerome lost its grip and has been slipping out of Cleopatra's lap ever since. Some buildings slowly fall inward, timbers flung out like arms, tall-crowned roofs tilted like ten-gallon hats. Each structure looks like a loser in an Old West shoot-out that time stopped in mid-slump. The jail bolted, made a break for it, escaping by the inch until it now sits more than 200 feet from its original site. Nearby, a Mexican Methodist church, built of sturdier stuff—dynamite powder boxes—held its ground.

Jerome has come back to life. Currently in a boom of restoration, the town is home to some 500 people, many of them artists and writers; all, the adventurous, the independent. I climbed up and slid down Jerome's streets, cautiously negotiating a sidewalk so as not to fall out into the sky. Buildings seemed to be stacked one upon the other, like cards and matchsticks.

"It's the only place I've ever seen," said one visitor, "where you can throw your dishwater out the back door and down your neighbor's chimney." I followed the steep road out of Jerome. On the valley floor I gazed back up at the mountain. Cleopatra sat solemnly, wearing a tall hat made of storm. Quietly the wind, like a teasing friend in affectionate jest, crept from behind and tipped the storm forward, down over the jaunty face of Jerome.

As the cloud flies, Grief Hill looms not far away. There, in August 1865, a doctor, 4 broken-down mules, a wagon, 30 days' rations, and 19 soldiers met misfortune. The wagon wrecked on the sharp grade. Apaches burned the wagon and its contents, but the surviving military party pushed on and camped at Clear Creek, three miles from present-day Fort Verde. The post, occupied in 1870, tops a rise and commands a long view of the valley. Bob Munson, historian and archaeologist, has helped restore the fort's weathered buildings. We toured the doctor's quarters and bachelor officers' quarters and stood on the porch of the commanding officer's house to view the old parade ground. Bob pointed out that one reason the fort was built was to protect settlers and miners from marauding Indians. One troublesome band was led by Chief Cha-lipun, called Charley-Pan by the soldiers.

"It was on April 23, 1873, that General George Crook stood here," said Bob. "Cha-lipun, with 300 of his Indians, stood there on the parade ground. They had come to surrender." With Yavapai-Apache threats ended in the valley, Fort Verde was abandoned by 1891. Indians had made the peace they had first sought from the Spanish.

F Oaxaca

ar to the south in Mexico misty clouds drift down and nod against the earth as if to sleep. They envelop the mountains and fill the ravines and the valley with the promise of rain. The intimacy of these ethereal omens inspired ancient Oaxaca Indians of Mexico to call themselves the "Cloud People" and to look to their rain gods as supreme.

In the Mexican state of Oaxaca three valleys merge in an elongated Y-shape to form the Valley of Oaxaca some 300 miles south of Mexico City. Earthquakes still rock this fertile cradle, mainly a land of cornfields. This setting nurtured the princes and peasants of long-ago kingdoms, domains as unstable as the valley itself.

Zapotec kings ruled thousands of years after early inhabitants began farming the bountiful terrain. Around 200 B.C. some of these farmers rose to royalty to dominate the valley. With their complex calendar, writing system, and architectural skill, they formed one of Mesoamerica's most advanced civilizations. They built palaces and temples massive in scale; they made sculptures larger than life. By cutting away rock and filling in with dirt, the Zapotecs flattened part of a mountaintop at the   (Continued on page 137)

Roofless walls of mud and stone mark Tuzigoot, a pre-Columbian pueblo in Arizona. Harsh living conditions forced Indians to abandon the site around 1400. Today a copper plant's settling pond fans out below the weathered ruins.

*L*ooking
deceptively stable,
Cleopatra Hill offers
a precarious perch for
buildings in Jerome,
Arizona. Mud slides
and years of miners
blasting tunnels into
its steep slopes have
weakened Cleopatra.
The hill occasionally
shudders, causing
some of Jerome's
buildings to shift. At
the turn of the century
the mining town had
a reputation as a
violent, wicked copper
camp. After the last
mine closed in 1953,
Jerome nearly
became a ghost town.
Rediscovered and now
being restored, Jerome
treats residents to
Verde Valley's clean
air and sweeping
views of red-rock
country and distant,
snow-clad peaks.

S*culptured saints occupy niches above the entrance of the cathedral in Oaxaca, the largest city in Mexico's Oaxaca Valley. Soon after the Spanish took control of the valley in 1521, Dominican missionaries overlaid Indian religions with Christian practices and trained native artisans to build ornate churches and monasteries. Gilded cupola (opposite) gleams inside Oaxaca's Church of Santo Domingo. Medallions display friars and winged angels rising toward a golden dove, symbol of the Holy Spirit, at the apex of the dome.*

Legacy of craftsmanship spans generations in the Valley of Oaxaca. Potter Luis García Blanco shapes figures in the style developed by his late mother, Doña Teodora, a famed artisan in the village of Atzompa. By his father's side, self-appointed apprentice Teodoro Luis, 3, fashions small cups from black clay that lightens in color when fired.

FOLLOWING PAGES: *Aged Mexican laurels shade a farmer and his oxen in San Francisco Javier, once a flourishing hacienda in the Valley of Oaxaca. In the 1500s the Spanish divided some of the valley's Indian lands into grand estates. To work the fertile tracts, the Spaniards introduced to Mexico such farming innovations as the ox-drawn plow.*

*O*vergrown with scrub brush, palaces and temples of Monte Albán weather the centuries
in the Valley of Oaxaca. Zapotecs built the mountaintop city and founded one of Mesoamerica's
most astonishing civilizations. Abandoned about A.D. 750, Monte Albán later became a sacred
necropolis. Stone carvings (far left) may depict early Zapotecs. A gold pectoral (left), part
of a tomb offering crafted in the style of the Mixtec Indians, may represent a deity.

confluence of the valleys to build a sacred city, Monte Albán. About A.D. 700 as many as 30,000 people may have lived in the capital's three square miles of mountainside sprawl. The heart of Monte Albán enclosed domestic and religious compounds used by royalty. Buildings have been restored at the site's center, but most of the city remains unexcavated. I saw large masonry buildings buried in earthen hillocks, and I viewed narrow terraces of simple dwellings half hidden by soil and vegetation. The valley and its heights hold many such ruins. Some are the fragments of cities occupied by the Mixtecs, rivals of the Zapotecs.

By 1400 Monte Albán had become a city of the dead—a sacred necropolis for rulers and commoners. Some tombs contained lavish offerings—sculptures and ceramic vessels, depicting massive jaguars and imposing deities. One of the burial chambers, Tomb 7, yielded the greatest treasure find in North America. In January 1932 Mexican archaeologist Alfonso Caso opened the tomb and saw ". . . in the center of a great pile of bones, glittered objects of gold. . . . Strung on the arm bones of one of the skeletons were ten bracelets, six of gold and four of silver." The tomb contained nine burials and more than 500 objects, including pearls, pieces of turquoise, and a golden diadem.

New invaders subjugated the Mixtecs and Zapotecs; the Aztecs dominated the valley by 1500. Zapotecs and Mixtecs alike paid tribute—and occasionally resisted. Then the Spanish arrived in 1521 to subdue all. The conquistador Hernán Cortés considered the valley such a prize that he made it a part of his personal domain. The Spaniards overlaid Indian heritage with their own. Today Oaxaca remains a cultural mix. Conversations change from Spanish to Indian languages and back again in mid-gossip. Listeners hear the whispering voices of Mixtec; Zapotec's "hissing murmurs." Writer D. H. Lawrence said of the market: "It sounds as if all the ghosts in the world were talking to one another, in ghost-voices, within the darkness of the market structure. It is a noise something like rain, or banana leaves in a wind."

Indians gather for market in the city of Oaxaca in dress emblazoned with bright designs that identify their home villages. Food stalls may offer steaming pork or beef, foods introduced by Spaniards, but flavored with Indian herbs and spices and wrapped in the ubiquitous tortilla—the flat bread as ancient as tradition. Vendors display woven blankets and embroidered clothes, pottery by the aisle, baskets by the mound.

Residents of the Valley of Oaxaca worship in churches of Spanish origin and design, but vestiges of the earlier religions remain. In Teotitlán del Valle, a village of weavers, I saw ancient carvings incorporated into the colonial church facade. An Indian warrior brandishes a spear; glyphs record prehistoric events. A stone cross centers small chapels in the four corners of the courtyard, a re-creation of the ancient concept of the four directions of the universe and its center. It is said ancient people of Teotitlán worshiped a sun god who came to earth in the form of a bird.

Teotitlán del Valle is a textile center so old that it was paying a tribute of cotton mantles to rulers 600 years ago. The village square and streets are festooned with woolen textiles for sale. I stood at the gate of a weaver's house.

Swirling a salute to history, a dancer in the traditional lace-trimmed dress of Oaxaca balances dahlias and daisies during Lunes de Cerro. This annual July festival celebrates the founding of the city by the Spanish crown in 1532.

"With your permission," I called. "Pass," came the reply. The family of José Montaño Sanchez led me through a patio and into the kitchen-dining room where flickering candles illuminated altar saints. José unfolded a gallery of woven designs: birds, butterflies, flowers, geometric patterns.

"These are old styles," José said, as he directed my attention to a blanket with a large flower, and another with a jaguar in mid-stride. But many of the geometric designs are older still—centuries older, for they appear on the facades of buildings at Mitla, an ancient religious center a few miles southeast of Teotitlán. Weavers in Teotitlán also copy gods and kings from the ancient codices—painted books of the Mixtecs and their contemporaries. "We are always experimenting here to see what nature will produce," José said. He showed me a weaving of a bird in flight and explained the sources of the natural dyes. The bird's yellow wings had come from orange peel, the rose and pink body and tail from oak bark. An array of browns had been derived from pecans and coffee beans. Touches of deep red had come from cochineal; these insects were so valued for dye in pre-Columbian and Spanish times that they made Oaxaca wealthy in trade.

In village after village I saw artisans' pride in craft. To find a wood-carver, I took a dusty road that followed an arroyo along the shadow of Monte Albán. I passed shepherd boys who were laughing and running as they tended leaping, skipping goats. The youngsters' lives echo the childhood of many Oaxaqueños, not the least Manuel Jiménez, a wood-carver in the village of Arrazola. He is a dignified man, and he spoke easily of his life and art.

"My father was Mixtec, my mother Zapotec. The Zapotecs are a very intelligent race. Because of this I am very intelligent. We were poor when I was a child. I cared for our animals. I stayed with them in cold, in heavy rain. I suffered. While I watched after them I began to work with clay I found in the fields, forming the shapes of the animals. There were no schools here. I taught myself to read and write almost overnight. It was almost a kind of miracle. I never had a teacher for reading or wood carving.

"To make something from one's mind, to create an original, is an inspiration. God opens the doors of the heart. Because of this there is a mystery within each animal I carve. That mystery is what makes it increase in value, makes it legitimate. Everyone has a destiny. I have found mine in my art." Manuel chuckled. "One man's destiny may be dancing with beautiful women. But when the music stops, his destiny ends. Mine always goes on."

Manuel proudly showed his work: a chunk of wood had become a reclining jaguar with magenta ears; a curved limb had changed into a purple coyote. He readied a shipment of *naguals*, spirit-animals with human heads, for a Philadelphia gallery and fondly recalled exhibits in Los Angeles and Austin. "But I still farm, plant some corn. I like to be close to the land," he said.

Oaxaca farmers, by necessity, depend on nature's whims, helped or hindered by the supernatural. Jesus descends in the afternoons to bless crops, but devils lie in wait at crossroads. Witches endanger adults and children alike, and La Llorona—the Woman Who Weeps—is the devil disguised as a beautiful woman who seduces her victims, then maims them. Zapotecs deal directly with a hostile world of supernatural beings. Collectively tense and anxiety-ridden, the Indians are sometimes victims in a vulnerable land.

The summer rains had not come. Cornstalks stood beige and brittle in the fields. A woman gazed at me in unconcealed alarm. "This is a beautiful place, but an unlucky place," she began. "We will die of hunger, of thirst. The rain does not want to fall. It was the same last year. It is from God. He is angry with us. We have behaved badly. The crops are drying. They will not ripen. It is the time of fruit trees. The fruit comes very tiny. They need water. There is no grass for the cattle. Some say it is from nature; I believe it is from God. The countries that don't suffer from hunger have war. What will we do?" I had no answer, but that afternoon I stood on a mountainside and watched without surprise as two dark rainstorms linked by a rainbow swept across the valley.

Querétaro

Supernatural happenings appeared commonplace in the lives of Indians and Spaniards throughout Mexico in the 16th century. So a miracle of conquest in the valley of Querétaro, some 400 miles north of Oaxaca, came as no surprise. Tradition says that on July 25, 1531, as Spaniards and their Otomí Indian allies battled Chichimec Indian warriors in hand-to-hand combat, the sun disappeared and bright stars shone. It is said that a glowing cross and the image of Saint James, Spain's champion against the Moors, appeared in the sky. The Spaniards took it as a sign from heaven that divine providence was on their side. History does not record what the Chichimecs took the "mystical happenings" for, nor how they recognized the portent, but they thought it best to surrender immediately and did so without further resistance.

The valley of Querétaro lies in a central mesa province between Mexico's two Sierra Madre ranges. Defined by long, low hills, the valley makes up part of the vast Bajío Plateau—the breadbasket of Mexico. Under Spanish rule Querétaro became a center of farming, mining, and wool manufacturing; wealth and religious fervor transformed the city of Querétaro into an architectural jewel now enclosed in a modern setting. It is a place that honors tradition. Rather than tear down historic buildings, the city developed new suburbs and industries around its colonial core. More than a hundred factories, many of them subsidiaries of U. S. companies, ring Querétaro. Laws ban traffic from the city's narrow streets—passageways paved in pink sandstone, the same pastry-tint material used in many of the original houses, government buildings, churches, and monasteries.

On midday strolls sunlight bounces a blinding glare from the old facades. Stone escutcheons, carved over massive wooden doorways and defaced after one of the country's many revolutions, once proclaimed houses of nobility. Fanciful iron balconies and grilles on shuttered windows remind of romance and intrigue. Resplendent domes, Moorish tiles, tiers, garlands, cherubs, and saints on convoluted gilt altars hint of the intricacies and ecclesiastical pomp of the Spanish Renaissance. Dark leaves of laurels shade quiet parks where sculptures of prominent men preside and stone animals lean down and spew water into splashing fountains.

Credit for many of Querétaro's most striking 18th-century buildings goes to architect Ignacio Mariano de las Casas. The house that he designed for himself, the House of the Dogs, captures the imaginative personality of the man. Stone dogs recline along the outside gutters. A smiling teacher opened the door to let me into a patio of laughter, for the building is now a federal kindergarten. Stone masks, dogs, and gargoyles gazed as children scrambled over winged beasts on the central fountain. To one side of the courtyard stood a miniature medieval castle with crenellated walls, tiny staircases, and child-scale doors. Some believe de las Casas designed the castle for his children, but documents mention only a wife. It may be the work of a man who was child enough to dream and man enough to fulfill his fantasies.

Within a few days young Luz María Contreras showed me much of the history of Mexico. At ease with the past, Luz is a delicately serene daughter of classical Spanish families. "This is the most beautiful place to me," Luz said as we stood on Sangremal Hill, where the miraculous conquest of the Chichimecs took place. Spaniards had built the Church and Convent of the Cross here in gratitude. Inside the complex, Luz and I climbed worn stone stairs, wandered thick-walled passages, and paused in a patio to examine trees bearing cross-shaped thorns—which local people say are yet one more miracle. It was at this convent that Father Junípero Serra stayed while en route to convert Indians and to build chains of missions as far away as California. In this same convent Emperor Maximilian spent his first days as a prisoner in May 1867, in a room as stark as a monk's cell.

Benito Juárez had been president when the French intervened and enthroned the Austrian archduke Maximilian as Mexico's emperor. Maximilian's chapel on the Hill of the Bells overlooks Querétaro, but a huge statue of Juárez looms behind it and dominates all. An illiterate Zapotec shepherd boy from the mountains of Oaxaca, Juárez learned to read at age 12, went on to study law, and became the stern savior of his country. On the edge of Querétaro, on the Hill of the Bells, Maximilian surrendered to the rebel troops of Juárez, and Mexico again assumed self-rule.

A small chapel of pink stone marks the place of Maximilian's surrender and later execution. Luz and I peered though metal grilles to see three stones that mark where Maximilian and two of his generals stood before a firing squad. The tragic ruler had spoken kindly to his executioners, absolved them of guilt, and awarded each a gold coin known as a Maximilian.

Few countries have heroines as well loved as Mexico's La Corregidora, Doña Josefa Ortiz de Domínguez. In 1810 her husband—Querétaro's magistrate—or *corregidor*—locked her in a room after he had discovered her role in a conspiracy of revolt against Spanish rule. She alerted a co-conspirator by tapping her heels on the floor. Through a keyhole she passed a warning that her husband intended to quell the uprising. Her ally spread the alarm, and so began the successful revolution. A statue of La Corregidora shares the heights above Querétaro with the likeness of Juárez.

To see more of the valley of Querétaro, Luz and I drove toward Villa del Pueblito. At the edge of the town we stopped near a tall pyramid, already ancient when the Spaniards arrived. The time-worn landmark is known locally as Cerro Pelón, Bald Hill. Its rubble sides lead to a stone mansion with empty Gothic windows and a collapsed roof, its rooms *(Continued on page 146)*

This stark cell—part of the Convent of the Cross in the valley of Querétaro—imprisoned Maximilian, an Austrian who became Mexico's emperor. Mexico regained self-rule after troops of Benito Juárez defeated Maximilian in 1867.

G overnment Palace in Querétaro once seethed with intrigue. Planning a revolt against Spanish rule, rebels met here often with Doña Josefa Ortiz de Domínguez (far right), wife of the Spanish magistrate, or corregidor. Her husband discovered the plot and locked her in a

room. *Summoning a co-conspirator by tapping her heels, she passed a warning through the keyhole. The alarm set off a successful revolution in 1810. Today Mexico lauds Querétaro as the "cradle of independence" and La Corregidora as its heroine.*

Beyond the city's aqueduct, domes and spires of churches and monasteries
command the skyline of Querétaro. Legend says that a marquis, enamored
of a beautiful nun, granted her wish for fresh water by building the aqueduct.
Completed in 1735, it carried spring water to public fountains. Wealth

from mines, wool manufacturing, and agriculture financed construction of the city, today considered a showplace of colonial architecture. The Treaty of Guadalupe Hidalgo, signed in Querétaro in 1848, ended the war between the U. S. and Mexico and ceded Mexican territory that later became New Mexico, Arizona, California, Nevada, Utah, and part of Colorado.

now open to the sky. A man was so jealous of his beautiful bride that he built this house to keep anyone from seeing her, claims a popular legend.

"A nice romantic story," Professor Eduardo Loarca, director of the regional museum said. "But a more truthful version is that he probably built the house so he could watch workers in the fields below. He was a hacienda owner with old-fashioned ideas. He died half crazy at the turn of the century."

Legend and truth blended long ago to enhance the pyramid. In his office on Pueblito's plaza, Municipal President Rodolfo Valdez Mora told us more. "Pueblito was a religious center in ancient times. This tradition continues. The Virgin Mary appeared here. And twice each year people perform religious dances at the foot of the pyramid. They feast and exchange gifts."

I could picture them there. Some dress as Christians, some as Moors. They sway and whirl in dramatic firelight to the sound of flute and drum. I wondered about the rites performed when the pyramid was new and homage paid to forgotten gods. And I thought about the half-mad *hidalgo*. Had he silently watched his laborers worship as well as work nearly a century ago?

One of the most moving sights in Querétaro for an American is the elaborate gilt table in the regional museum; it was on this table, with flourishes of a pen, that much of northern Mexico became part of the United States. With the Treaty of Guadalupe Hidalgo in 1848 the U. S.-Mexican War ended, and Mexico ceded territory that later became Arizona, New Mexico, California, Nevada, Utah, and part of Colorado. Those signatures opened places like the Verde Valley for Anglo-American settlers.

T Middle Rio Grande

wo and a half centuries before the cession of New Mexico, Spanish explorers and colonists had beaten a track called the Camino Real northward into the middle Rio Grande Valley. This area, a land of contrasts, runs from El Paso, Texas, to Albuquerque, New Mexico. It's often a land of dry wind, burning sun, and parched lips—a place made green by the river that meanders along a path of fertility. It's a valley dotted with cactus, creosote bush and, along the waterways, salt cedar and cottonwood. It's a desert relieved by soothing hot springs and checkered with irrigated fields, vineyards, and orchards. It's a place where history lives.

One of the historical figures is Juan de Oñate. A wealthy man of influence, he married Cortés's granddaughter, who was also the great-granddaughter of the Aztec emperor Moctezuma II. He won permission to colonize the territory of New Mexico. In April of 1598 he reached the Rio Grande about 40 miles south of present-day El Paso with 400 men, 130 families, 83 wagons and carts of baggage, and more than 7,000 head of livestock. It had been a hard journey of more than two months from the banks of the Rio Conchos north across the Chihuahuan Desert. I covered the same route in less than five hours by train, and I seldom took my eyes from the slowly changing scenes.

Stretching northward from Mexico City, the irrigated plain of the Bajío gives onto desert flats broken by mountains of rock and sand. Distant stone and adobe villages spill down hillsides that seem to shimmer in the heat. At times a long expanse of parched countryside breaks into a fleeting glimpse of an isolated ranch. Clusters of modest buildings gain shade from a few trees, while a slow windmill grinds out trickles of water.

Oñate had led his colonists through such terrain and up the mountain-edged corridor that is the middle Rio Grande Valley, a land that he saw as "a possession so good that none other of his Majesty in these Indies excells it. . . ." Many would disagree with such an exaggerated appraisal. A governor more than a hundred years later gave a realistic view of colonial hardship when he wrote to an official in Mexico City: "For the love of God and Saint Anthony . . . do everything you possibly can to get me out of here."

The Spanish settlers discovered villages of helpful Pueblo Indians, and the Spaniards overlaid their customs, as did the Anglo-Americans later. The middle Rio Grande Valley became a cultural mix. A northbound chain of place-names in New Mexico recalls both trials and blessings of Spaniards during early settlement: Las Cruces, supposedly named for the cross-marked graves of newcomers killed by the Indians; Jornada del Muerto, Journey of Death, for a 90-mile mountain bypass whose scant supplies of water posed a hazard for animals and humans; Sevilleta, which conjured diminutive memories of home and Seville; and Socorro—help, succor—for a place where Pueblo Indians gave food and drink to Spaniards in need of aid.

The Organ Mountains are perhaps the middle valley's most impressive peaks. They loom on the horizon near Las Cruces. North of the city, the Rio Grande bends westward. Here began the Journey of Death. This route, part of the Camino Real, enabled wagons and carts to skirt the Fra Cristobal Range and the Caballo Mountains. In 1847 Susan Shelby Magoffin, a trader's wife, joined her husband's caravan, traveling the Jornada by night and resting through the hottest hours, as was the custom. She noted: "The country is quite level immediately around us, with dark hills in the distance. The grass is short and dry, the soil sandy . . . and the whole puts on a gloomy aspect. . . . It is really dangerous. We are in the heart of the Apache range. . . ."

The treacherous route gave its name, Jornada del Muerto, to the desert country that covers some 2,000 square miles southeast of Socorro. Today the Jornada includes part of the northwest corner of the White Sands Missile Range, the place where the first atomic bomb was exploded.

If any corner of the valley has witnessed southwestern drama, it is the area around the present town of Mesilla. Apaches roamed here, and conquistadores, colonists, and trade caravans passed by on the Camino Real. The town began as a Mexican village. The Gadsden Purchase made Mesilla part of the U. S. in 1854 and established New Mexico's southern border. In 1861 the town served as a Confederate headquarters during the Civil War.

Gunslingers and cavalry troopers roamed the town square and dusty streets of Mesilla. The town was a major stop for the Butterfield Stage, which linked Fort Smith, Arkansas, with San Francisco. The adobe building that served as the depot still stands on a narrow side street. "The most murderous youth that ever stood in shoe leather," William H. Bonney—Billy the Kid—swaggered into Mesilla's gambling halls and saloons. East of the town, near the Organ Mountains, a gunman bushwhacked sheriff Pat Garrett, the man who finally killed Billy the Kid.

One common foe feared by gunslingers, Pueblo Indians, and settlers alike was the Apache. The territory of these Indians had been taken. Unable to live off the land, the Apaches lived off the interlopers. In 1865 Fort Selden was established at the southern entrance of the Jornada del Muerto for protection. One morning in bright sunshine I strolled along one of the fort's graveled pathways. Around me stood crumbled adobe walls. Military markers cited life in the valley a century ago. Gen. Douglas MacArthur spent almost two years of his childhood here. His father, Capt. Arthur MacArthur, commanded the fort from 1884 to 1886. Here the museum displays uniforms, trappings of daily life, weapons, and a machine that helped break the Apaches.

In the late 1800s a system of heliographs, or sun telegraphs, began at Fort Selden and blinked across Arizona as far as Fort Verde and beyond. Messages and warnings flashed from mountaintop to mountaintop, from fort to fort. The Chiricahua Apache chief Geronimo supposedly said: "If the white man can speak with light, the Indian can do little. Our day is finished." At last, in 1886, Geronimo surrendered to Gen. Nelson A. Miles in southeastern Arizona and ended his days as a curious exhibit in fairs.

The Apaches had been at home in the Jornada del Muerto, familiar with every peak and ravine. I drove into the desert from Truth or Consequences, a town once named Hot Springs for the relaxing bath waters the Apaches favored there. At the end of the paved road I discovered that the settlement marked on the map as Engle contained two adobe buildings facing each other, as if to form a town. No one was there. I heard not a sound except a tough and lonely wind across sere mountains. I walked for a time in the miles of rock and sand on a treeless plain. Wild flowers bloomed in the wilting heat, but I saw no movement of animal life. From somewhere, at last, came the song of a bird. The sunbaked expanse made the world seem so arid that it was hard to imagine that New Mexico's largest body of water lay not far beyond the distant mountains. Created by damming the Rio Grande, Elephant Butte Reservoir at its high watermark covers 36,000 acres.

"Elephant Butte was one of the first great irrigation systems in the West," historian Paige Christiansen of the New Mexico Institute of Mining and Technology told me as we stood on the banks of the Rio Grande at Socorro. We watched the sand-colored river hurtle past, rising by the minute from heavy snowmelt in the distant Rockies. In places the water came to within inches of the top of the bank, undercutting miniature sandy cliffs and adding to the silt it swept along. Low-lying areas had already begun to flood.

"I've been here 25 years, and I've never seen the river this high," Dr. Christiansen said. "We have a great deal of water underground, but not much surface water."

Millions of years ago in this region of the Southwest the mountains uplifted. Segments of the earth subsided and created a series of basins that became the middle Rio Grande Valley. But the passing ages slowly filled the gorge with sediment. "Take the gravel out of this valley, and you would have a Grand Canyon," Dr. Christiansen said.

Today Socorro maintains its 19th-century flavor, which stems from a cultural blend of Hispanic and American. "We're still a minority-majority town—60 percent Spanish speakers," Dr. Christiansen said. Gold and silver strikes gave life to Socorro in the late 1800s. Those were the days of gambling halls and hanging trees, times when drinking water had to be carried down from mountain springs and roots were sometimes wrenched from the earth for fuel. As an Anglo murderer stood beneath a cottonwood tree that would serve as his gibbet, his last words were of the harsh land, the foreign customs, and the relief that he felt at leaving it. "It's a damn tough country where you have to climb for water, dig for wood, and they call corn 'mice' [Spanish, *maíz*]. I'll take my medicine like a little man."

I found many traces of old Spain in the valley. In his office in Belen, Magistrate Gil Sanchez, a courtly man, and his gracious wife, Priscilla, told me of their ties to the valley. "Our families go back to the Spanish land grants," Mr. Sanchez said. "Priscilla's family has documents from the 1600s."

"My great-grandfather was scalped by Indians," Priscilla said. "I grew up near where it happened—on my grandparents' sheep ranch in the mountains. I used to help with the lambing. When I was 13, my dad brought me here to Belen. He thought I should go to a school. But what a wonderful education I had already! I lived in the mountains with nature all around me."

Mr. Sanchez's nephew, Father Albert Gallegos, shares a musical accent heard in the valley, English tinged with the sound of the Spanish tongue. "We use 16th-century words—ancient words that are no longer spoken even in Spain—words Cervantes used in *Don Quixote*," Father Albert said. "We also honor religious customs practiced by Spaniards centuries ago."

At the settlement of Veguita we met a group of Penitentes, members of a lay brotherhood. It was the day before Good Friday, and we found the brothers readying their *morada*, or meetinghouse, for ceremonies. La Muerte— Death—a carved wooden skeleton shrouded in black—lay in a coffin near the altar. One of the brothers explained the figure: "It's to remind us that death is the sacrifice we will all endure. What is important is the soul."

"No visitors tomorrow. No photographs at our ceremonies," the brothers said firmly. "We just want to be left alone. We do not show off what we do. We pray for you, other people, ourselves. We are just serving our Lord." Behind the morada we climbed a sandy path the color of dark gold. It led up a long hill. White crosses lined the path on either side. At the top stood a taller cross silhouetted against the distant Manzano Mountains, their sharp ridges and deep ravines powdered by light snow. Penitentes once practiced self-flagellation, but no more, Father Albert said. As we neared the crest of the hill, he added: "Change is inevitable. Not many young people become Penitentes, but I doubt it will die out. It is a very strong part of our culture. It's a protection in a harsh life."

Good Friday dawned bright and clear, and I thought of the brothers and their shadowed rites. That afternoon, day suddenly changed into night. The darkness of a dust storm swept in from the west. A strong wind moaned across the valley. Desert sand blew in spirals that resembled entwined apparitions rising. Balls of tumbleweed bounded, floated up, and crashed to earth without a whisper. Outlines of buildings blurred, and the mountains faded until the valley became a featureless sea of swirling sand.

The sting of the gritty air reminded me that the waves of people who struggled to make these lands their own have all been fragile, and the centuries transient moments in the scheme of things. The drama ends, and silence pervades, but the setting remains. It is the valleys that endure.

FOLLOWING PAGES: *An arid plain in the Jornada del Muerto basin lies alongside New Mexico's middle Rio Grande Valley. In 1945 at Trinity Site, located near the pale oval area beyond the arroyos, the first atomic bomb was detonated.*

B ell-shaped blossoms of a yucca and bare peaks of the Organ Mountains dramatize the beauty of the middle Rio Grande Valley. Four-toed tracks on a sand dune (right) in New Mexico reveal the presence of roadrunners in the Sevilleta National Wildlife Refuge.

FOLLOWING PAGES: *At evening prayer, Edwin Berry lightly touches a cross at the crest of a hill near Tome, New Mexico. Edwin erected these crosses—which symbolize Calvary— in the tradition of the Penitentes, a lay religious brotherhood. The Penitentes observe Good Friday with secret rites rooted in medieval Spain. Publicity shy, the brothers find that their strict beliefs blend well with the rigorous terrain of the middle Rio Grande Valley.*

THE PACIFIC REACHES

Text by Jane R. McCauley/Photographs by Richard A. Cooke III

Kohala

Late one evening in the darkness of a raging Hawaiian storm, a figure embracing a newborn child sped along rocky cliffs hundreds of feet above the churning sea. Across the western sky a star traced a fiery path, an omen to all the kings that a rebel chief had been born.

The year, historians speculate, was 1758, and the child, Kamehameha I. Eventually the warrior would unify the Hawaiian Islands. Learning of a plot to kill her infant son, Kamehameha's mother entrusted him to a local chief who carried the baby deep into the mountains of Kohala. She knew that there, in the secluded valleys of the region, the young ruler would be safe.

For centuries Hawaiians found natural homelands in the valleys of Kohala. Born of the fire of a volcano more than 700,000 years ago, the Kohala Mountains probe some 20 miles northwestward across the far corner of the state's largest island of Hawaii. Chiseled by wind and water, seven richly forested valleys slice into the eastern flank of the mountains, widening and deepening in places before they dip into the transparent waters of the Pacific Ocean. Often mist and fog shroud the realm, one of the wettest in the archipelago, and winds rush about ceaselessly in its vastness.

This particular summer I would enter Kohala and explore the valleys of Pololu, Honokane Iki, and the region of Awini. Then I would travel east to Owens Valley in California, then northward to Fraser Valley in British Columbia, and finally to the Matanuska Valley in Alaska. Though geographically diverse, all are steeped in folklore and populated by true individualists. In all my ramblings, though, I would find Kohala's valleys to be the least charted, and for me, the most physically demanding.

The best introduction to the area, I learned, was by air. Dr. Augustine Furumoto, a professor of geophysics at the University of Hawaii in Honolulu, enlightened me as we flew past cliffs stippled in every conceivable shade of green. "Some of them reach 1,400 feet," Dr. Furumoto said. "Before erosion took its toll, the cliffs were higher."

We swooped low, hugging the dark ribbon of shoreline. "The black sand you see below," Dr. Furumoto said, "occurs when hot lava hits cool water. The island of Hawaii was created from five volcanoes; Kohala volcano formed first. Its eastern slope eroded into the valleys you're going to visit."

Climbing higher we banked and then cruised along the coast. Waterfalls bounded from bluffs and toppled in thin, silvery plumes for hundreds of feet; I could almost hear their roar. If I were a bird, I thought, I could soar far and wide in these intriguing recesses, alighting on the shimmery kukui trees and splashing in the clear streams. Had I found a Shangri-la, I wondered.

Misty ocean breezes bathe volcanic cliffs along the northeast coast of Hawaii, the youngest island in the Hawaiian chain. Mountains shield seven valleys in a region called Kohala. Throughout the reaches of the Pacific, valleys beckon with a diversity ranging from tropical lushness to desert starkness.
PRECEDING PAGES: *Fog sweeps across the Fraser Valley in British Columbia.*

"They say Kohala is a big coffeepot that held all the people at one time, pouring them out to neighboring islands," Cheri Sproat said one evening as we discussed the Hawaiian culture. "Almost everyone in the islands can trace his ancestry back to the Kohala region," she added. Her husband, Clyde, agreed. He grew up in one of these valleys, as did his grandmother, father, and brother. But Clyde's roots reach even deeper. His great-grandmother inherited the Pololu Valley from Hawaiian royalty. Now Clyde had agreed to share his heritage with me. We talked in the kitchen of the Sproats' home on a hillside at the Pololu Lookout, a site that marks the entrance to the valley. The glow of an oil lamp etched a jar of leathery, red anthuriums on the kitchen counter. I turned and looked out the window at a solitary tree jutting in the moonlight on a distant ridge. I knew that tomorrow, with Cheri and Clyde, I would journey to that far sentinel.

The next morning I mounted Pika (a surefooted horse, Clyde assured me) and fell in line behind Cheri and their friend Eddie. Clyde, his tanned, bald head covered with a faded red bandanna, rode behind with a heavily laden pack mule. In single file we started down the Kohala Ditch Trail. For 55 miles, up and down mountain slopes and across five valleys, the path winds southeastward from Pololu Lookout. The trail takes its name from the Kohala Ditch Company, a venture first envisioned after seven worry-filled months in 1897. During that time not a drop of rain fell in the Kohala District. Wind-stripped sugarcane shriveled in parched fields.

From his home an imaginative planter named John Hind gazed out at the numerous streamlets and waterfalls crisscrossing the mountains. He dreamed of harnessing those water sources. That vision—together with several unsuccessful attempts at overhead irrigation—spurred him and two other planters to form the Kohala Ditch Company in 1904. It took almost two years of exhausting work to dig the 21-mile-long network of tunnels and ditches. Tools and supplies had to be carried up sheer cliffs. Most of the tunnels cut through the range's basalt walls were chiseled out by hand. When completed, the ditch channeled about 35 million gallons of water daily down forested slopes and across flat valley floors to the cane fields.

Finding a way through the valleys along the many service trails that parallel portions of the ditch seems easy for Clyde. His grandfather, father, and brother were all superintendents with the Kohala Ditch Company; Clyde, or "Kindy" as his friends call him, can scamper up and down the cliffs with the ease of a mountain goat. Creeping ferns and stubborn weeds have overtaken many sections of the Kohala Ditch Trail, which reverted to wilderness after the area's last sugar mill closed in 1975. No permanent residents remain in the region. A large corporation maintains portions of the switchback trail; most of it, however, is nearly impenetrable, and even for the seasoned hiker it's safer by animal than on foot.

Our descent into Pololu was precarious from the start. Pika bumped and lurched in the jumble of stones covering the steep, 450-foot-long path. Fear jostled its way to the front of my mind, and I called out to Cheri. "Is it like this the whole way?"

"Oh no," she replied mischievously. "It gets much worse." I tightened my grip on the reins.

The trail led us down to a volcanic beach. Once across the clinging, black sand, we quickened our pace through a refreshingly cool grove of ironwood trees, the floor cushioned with their soft branchlets, then pushed farther into the hushed woods. A butterfly flittered by, its delicate orange wings disappearing in a maze of moist, curly fronds. Abruptly the trail narrowed to a mere foot in places, dissolving into nearly pathless undergrowth and a latticework of low-growing branches.

We bushwhacked, stooping to pass under toppled, decaying kukui trees as the animals hugged the unguarded edge of the cliffs. Heaps of splintered rocks slowed us. Once, I raised my head to reach for my notebook. Whack! Tenacious limbs snarled in my hair and grabbed at my face, sending the sunglasses resting on my head spiraling down over the cliff's edge. I remembered the warning Clyde's father had issued to me earlier of this place he calls the "eighth wonder of the world." He said: "If you fall over the side of one of those precipices, you'll starve to death before you reach the bottom." I resolved to pay closer attention.

As we plodded along, we nibbled on sweet rose apples, bits of moist coconut, and crimson thimbleberries—which taste like a blend of raspberries and strawberries. In his Hawaiian tongue Clyde sang hauntingly of evil men, broken hearts, and sandpipers. Near a clump of orchids a delicate white naupaka flower, precisely severed, caught my eye. Its other half, according to a legend, lives by the sea, a lover banished by a maiden for his unfaithfulness.

When we reached Honokane Iki, the second valley of our journey, we rested the animals. King Arthur could not have lived in a more idyllic setting. At the edge of a clearing, ringed on three sides by mountains and watered by a gentle creek, stood a little stone-and-wood house. Its cobweb-laced exterior reflected the fairy-tale atmosphere. Not far away, lofty coconut palms fringed an isolated cove cut by the ocean surf. I walked toward it and sat down on a mossy, aging root of an Indian fig tree. Clyde joined me.

"Cheri and I are going to live in that house," he said. Clyde's face mirrored the contentment of a soldier home at last. He spoke of his childhood days here, of the harsh "Maui" winds that can snap trees, and of the 1946 tsunami that altered the creek bed. The surf pounding on the beach turned my attention seaward. I thought about the Hawaiians who had lived here when Capt. James Cook discovered the islands in 1778. Access to the Pacific was critical to the natives. The ocean yielded an abundance of fish and provided the seafaring islanders a concourse for their canoes. Inland on terraced slopes the Hawaiians cultivated taro, from which they pounded poi, a staple food.

It was late afternoon when we reached Awini, about ten miles into the mountains. In this sheltered area, which contains several small valleys, the infant Kamehameha had found sanctuary more than 200 years ago. He spent several years in the Kohala region, where his training in the skills of leadership and warfare began. Kamehameha's triumphant reign, from 1791 to 1819, unified the Hawaiian Islands, encouraged foreign trade, and left the Hawaiian people a rich legacy of pride.

After nine hours of trekking across Kohala, I was tired and grubby. A dip in a cool brook, its banks spicy with white ginger, refreshed me. Clyde prepared a supper of hekka—a stew made with pork and taro, seasoned with ginger, garlic, and lemon juice. The pork came from a wild pig that Eddie had killed that day. After the feast, as I crawled into my sleeping bag, a far-off and eerie bellowing chilled my spine. "Wild bulls," Clyde muttered.

Huge bulls roam the cliffs of Kohala. The animals are descended from domesticated stock that belonged to workers of the Kohala Ditch Company. The bellowing of the beasts haunted me the next morning as we left Awini for our return to Clyde and Cheri's home. About a mile down the trail our animals halted unexpectedly. Curious, I arched my neck and stared into the black-and-white face of a bull. He stared right back with piercing, murderous eyes. We were trapped on a trail too narrow to turn around on. A sheer wall rose to our left and another plunged to our right. Our lives were at the mercy of a wild bull. I felt my throat tighten.

Minutes passed. Finally the animal lumbered off—up a cliff he alone could climb. I turned, shaking, and asked Clyde, "Would he have attacked?"

"You bet."

In the months to come I would often think of these enchanting, challenging, and sometimes frightening valleys of Kohala, "a place of destiny." I would remember foremost that Cheri had told Clyde that he could help me see this region through his eyes, but he could never show it to me through his heart. She's right, of course, but I know I share with him a mutual concern for preserving such wilderness legacies. For now, though, I could not linger; a valley of desert beauty in California beckoned.

Owens

For a long, long time the 80-foot-high granite monolith has stood on a crest to the east overlooking Owens Valley, waiting for the Great Spirit to release it. One popular legend holds that the imposing pillar was a Paiute Indian, named Winnedumah, who was transformed into stone when an enemy warrior cried out, "Stay right where you are."

Winnedumah Rock, scattered obsidian chips, and dozens of petroglyph sites are some of the few remaining clues to the early Paiutes. Clustered along streambeds, they lived mainly off piñon pine nuts. Some of the Indians also fished and combed meadows, hillsides, and forests for rabbits and other game. In the mid-1800s many of the Paiutes were forced to leave their villages when white settlers began claiming land in the valley.

From its uppermost point just north of the town of Bishop to its southernmost reaches at the community of Olancha, Owens Valley dramatically displays the work of land-molding forces. Earthquakes, volcanoes, wind, water, ice, and more recently man have all been artists in shaping this nearly hundred-mile-long channel. It runs between the angular Sierra Nevada and the more rounded Inyo and White Mountains. For more than three million years the valley has been sinking periodically as the mountains have been rising. Between these bulky ranges Owens drops more than two miles, one of the deepest troughs in the nation. At the same time the area claims the highest peak in the contiguous 48 states—14,494-foot Mount Whitney. To the west of the valley snow-covered Sierra slopes (Continued on page 175)

Exploring Pololu Valley, riders cross a black sand beach composed mainly of pulverized basalt from ancient volcanoes. Accessible only by sea and by narrow footpaths to early Hawaiians, the valleys of Kohala remain isolated realms.

Smooth branches of guava and leaves of hala trees canopy a rocky stream in Kohala's
Honokane Iki Valley. Raindrops bead a hapu'u *fern (below, left). A native of Honokane Iki,
Clyde Sproat (opposite) leads a party along the overgrown Kohala Ditch Trail. Hawaiians cut
the 55-mile path to service an irrigation system that supplied water to the area's sugarcane
fields. After the sugar industry withered in the 1970s, much of the trail reverted to wilderness.*

Beneath the Inyo Mountains in the Owens Valley of California, tule elk gather at dusk to forage in a nearby alfalfa field. Owens counts some 500 tule elk, the nation's largest concentration of these animals. Gnarled branches (right) rake the dry air in the Inyo's Ancient Bristlecone Pine Forest, a national preserve for these trees—possibly the world's oldest living things.

FOLLOWING PAGES: A dry corridor, Owens Valley separates snow-clad ranges: the Sierra Nevada, foreground, that raise peaks higher than 14,000 feet and the distant White and Inyo Mountains.

Across a sagebrush range, cowboys of the Lacey Ranch trail cattle from Owens Valley to Sierra pastures. Fed by scant rainfall and heavy snowmelt, Owens Lake sprawls in the distance. Weary after the drive, ranch hands (opposite) enjoy a breakfast in a mountain bunkhouse. Few ranchers remain in Owens Valley. Many cattlemen left in the early 1900s, after a Los Angeles group acquired property in the valley and began diverting its waters to the city.

"The loneliest land that ever came out of God's hands," wrote turn-of-the-century author Mary Austin of her birthplace, Owens Valley. Winter's melancholy weighs on the land. Bare poplars and Siberian elms fashion a tangled arch above a country lane (opposite) west of Bishop. Near Lone Pine, horses graze in a pasture made soggy by meltwater.

block moisture-laden clouds from Owens. The mountains also shelter the valley culturally from the more populated areas of the state. The identity of Owens can seem vague. Ask an urban Californian about the valley, and he may reply, as one did to me, "Oh, it's somewhere out there to the east where the rocks whisper, and no one can explain why."

Mysteries abound in this "land of little rain," as author Mary Austin called it. As she wrote and as I realized in time, "one must summer and winter with the land and wait its occasions." The valley is unpredictable. It changes from day to night, season to season, and in every direction.

Fed by chilly Sierra streams, the Owens River enters the valley northwest of Bishop, bypasses the town, and flows southward past arching cottonwoods, valley willows, and pasturelands. In early summer, west of Bishop, creeks swell from winter snows and tumble out of steep mountain canyons. A little farther south lie miles of desert scrub. Where ponds of meltwater and spring rain dry up, trees wither in parchment-like ground. At midday a gray haze moves in and hangs low, obscuring the point where ground and sky meet. Only grazing cattle interrupt the deathly stillness of the countryside.

Like many natives, Omie Mairs remembers an earlier time when fruit trees blossomed and creeks flooded meadows. He and his wife, Glorian, own a grocery store, its nooks and crannies filled with just about anything a person could want, including a warm, friendly smile. I sipped a cup of coffee with Omie early one Saturday morning in the cozy kitchen of his home in Independence, a sleepy town of some 700 about midway in the valley. Omie reflected on a bygone day of buggy rides, dirt roads, parlor games, and prospecting: "People here led a simple life, trout fishing, dancing, and playing cards. I'd stand outside my grandfather's hotel, and the miners would toss me a nickel. They were a bawdy bunch, but they had good hearts."

It was the discovery of mineral wealth in the 1860s that brought settlement to Owens Valley, more than a decade after gold fever had struck the rest of California. Lured by tales of great riches, the dreamers and the gullible drifted in from the west and Mexico, ushering in a romantic period filled with visions of a prosperous future. Loaded with silver bullion from the rich Cerro Gordo mine in the Inyos, steamers plied Owens Lake, which brimmed across 100 square miles at the valley's southern end. In the Sierra the Kearsarge mine shipped ore valued at $900 a ton. As mining camps created markets for grain, beef, and produce, farmers and cattlemen came. By the early 1900s irrigation water from the Owens River and artesian wells had made thousands of acres in the arid valley productive. Orchards of pears, peaches, and apples blossomed, and fields of corn, alfalfa, and wheat flourished.

"This was such a fertile place," Omie said. "The artesian wells outside of town really flowed." Today, except during extremely wet years, the dry bed of Owens Lake is crusty with salt crystals. Only a few farms punctuate the countryside, and a keen eye can discern a sprinkling of fruit trees clinging to life in abandoned orchards. Income from outdoor recreational activities in the mountains—such as hiking, skiing, and fishing—has surpassed earnings from ranching and farming, which once provided a livelihood for the region.

Banners of spring: Wild irises carpet a meadow bordered by the slopes of the Sierra Nevada west of Bishop. Despite little rainfall in the Owens Valley area, some 2,000 plant species bloom annually with a flourish of color.

The valley began to revert to a nonproductive basin after the completion of the Los Angeles aqueduct in the fall of 1913. A few years earlier, the abundant waters of the Owens River had caught the attention of a few men in Los Angeles. They believed that Owens Valley and its river could supply enough water for a burgeoning metropolis, as well as water for the irrigation of fields in the San Fernando Valley. The men purchased key property along the river. "I remember my grandparents were some of the first to sell," Omie told me without a trace of bitterness. "Imagine how they'd feel now."

By the end of 1913 the first aqueduct, an impressive engineering system, was carrying great volumes from the Owens. The deep blue waters flowed 234 miles along the edge of the stark Mojave Desert to the San Fernando Valley and Los Angeles. During the years of the Great Depression, Los Angeles acquired additional properties and now holds 308,500 acres in the valley and neighboring Mono County. A second aqueduct began carrying groundwater and additional surface water from the valley in 1970.

Just as earthquakes have redefined the landscape of Owens, the water controversy has structured, in many respects, the character of the valley's people. Sentiments run high in the decades-old battle. Everywhere I went—riding with a third-generation rancher to locate strays, sitting in a homey cafe, enjoying a lazy afternoon on the spacious porch of the Winnedumah Country Inn—people talked water.

One of the most outspoken is botanist Mary DeDecker, whose dedication to Owens Valley has prompted her to spend numerous hours preparing vegetation studies, writing newsletters, and working with a concerned citizens group. One morning, when a flawless sky seemed to unfold the immensity of the mountains before me, I set out with Mary to explore the altered landscape. At 74, dressed in jeans and tennis shoes, Mary is spry; I huffed and puffed to keep up with her.

We headed east along Mazourka Canyon Road toward the Inyos. Before crossing a section of the Los Angeles aqueduct, we paused at an artesian well. "People in this valley consider these wells a symbol of the issue," Mary said. Though now flowing, the well had been dry for much of the decade, partially a result of an increasing amount of groundwater being pumped to Los Angeles. The effects of the pumping were hard to ignore. "There, you see, that's greasewood." Mary pointed to a shriveled, thorny mass. "Groundwater is critical to its survival as well as the other desert plants."

Later I heard the other side of the issue. "By owning most of the land, Los Angeles has kept this valley uncluttered," one resident said. Another viewpoint supporting Los Angeles came from the northern district engineer for the aqueduct, Duane Buchholz. We had met in his office at the water department's valley headquarters in Bishop. Near me was a map of the area of Owens Valley and Mono Basin. The map displayed a rainbow of colored property holdings: white, the 4 percent in private hands; green and pink, the 93 percent that makes up the federal ownership of lands, mostly Inyo National Forest and Bureau of Land Management tracts; a wide swath of yellow, the 3 percent owned by Los Angeles.

"The real question," Duane said, "is how much are we affecting the natural vegetation and creating problems with air pollution by lowering the water table by the amount we do. For the first time," Duane said optimistically, "the people in the valley and the water department are working together, with

the U. S. Geological Survey as an objective third party. As a result we're drawing closer together toward an agreement on the amount of water that can safely be pumped from the valley."

Months later I learned that Los Angeles and Inyo County officials had agreed to negotiate a plan that would set the amount of groundwater to be drawn from the area. But even this preliminary accord has sparked new protests. Will the 80-year-old water controversy ever end, I wondered.

I had followed Highway 395 out of Owens Valley. The magic of the desert's setting sun turned the land into a Monet canvas of delicate pinks, lavenders, and greens against the gray mountains. Tule elk foraged, and jackrabbits scurried about. Life teemed in this valley, which I once thought so still. Far above me snow clogged Sierra passes, although July had come. My skin felt dry, my throat parched. "A land of lost rivers," Mary Austin had written, "with little in it to love; yet a land that once visited must be come back to inevitably. If it were not so there would be little told of it."

Fraser

Just as the beauty of Owens Valley lies in its desert starkness, the beauty of Canada's Fraser Valley in British Columbia lies in its gentle, well-watered lowlands and forested mountain slopes. From its eastern terminus at Hope to its western border at the Strait of Georgia, the valley displays a lush and pleasing landscape. In its one hundred miles it encompasses pastoral expanses, unspoiled forests of Douglas fir, western red cedar, and western hemlock, and calm rivers once navigated by stern-wheelers. Downstream, executives crowd skyscrapers, and tourists jam boutiques in Greater Vancouver—Fraser's metropolitan area of some one million people.

The valley is probably best understood through its river, and a passage along it can stir thoughts about the people who are prominent in the Fraser's history: from the Indians who harvested the river's fish to Scottish explorer Simon Fraser, from the gold seekers who panned the riverbed to the immigrants who put down roots along the Fraser's fertile floodplains. The river takes its name from Simon Fraser, who in 1808 led an expedition to the Fraser's mouth. Yet it remains an unhonored river. Few have witnessed its great moments, and none has praised its beauty or worth in song or saga.

High in the icy peaks of the Rockies, the waters of the Fraser begin their 850-mile journey. They plunge through gorges, swell as they merge with seven major tributaries, then seethe and squeeze through granite cliffs that line the river's awesome canyon. At Hope the Fraser turns westward, then subsides and flows through the valley's heartland. The watercourse cleaves fertile lowlands that reach to the foot of the Coast Mountains north of the Fraser and stretch beyond the Canadian border south of the river. Finally, in its maturity, the Fraser spawns a delta and beyond New Westminster spills into several channels that carry the river to the Strait of Georgia, part of Vancouver's waterway to the Pacific.

At Fort Langley National Historic Park, along the Fraser's south shore outside Vancouver, I learned more about the valley's heritage. The fort was

once part of the network of trading posts established by the Hudson's Bay Company in the early 1800s. It was here that the province of British Columbia was born on November 19, 1858. Gordon Yusko, the curatorial and archival services officer, showed me through the fort's five buildings. "The whole purpose of Fort Langley in the beginning was to undermine the American traders by controlling access to furs in the northern interior and by serving as a market for underselling competitors. In canoes made by the Salish Indians, supplies were shipped up the river to Fort Hope, and fur traders and their pelts came downriver in the boats. When fur trading grew unprofitable in the mid-1840s, the fort became a provision center. A farm and dairy were started. Later, miners stopped here before heading to the goldfields."

So began the area's agricultural and dairying tradition. It still thrives along the Fraser's banks, where tidy red-and-white barns front ridges traced by lucid skies and where cattle graze in emerald pastures and acres of leafy vegetables stand in ruler-straight rows. With the gold rush in 1858 came an increased demand for produce, which made market prices soar. Some 250 farms dotted these wide-open lowlands within the next decade. During the next century, immigrants—including English, Scotch, and Dutch—poured in, bringing with them European farming techniques that proved valuable in the new homeland. The settlers developed ways to manage the near sea-level ground, draining it in winter, irrigating it at times in summer, and diking it to control floodwaters that inundated it each spring.

To this day, dikes function up and down the river, as do many settlements. A number of the small populated areas cluster in the central part of the valley around the larger towns of Chilliwack and Abbotsford. Near Abbotsford I drove past raspberry fields and farmhouses. At the Ross farm I turned in.

June Ross met me near a Christmas-red barn trimmed in whitewash and decorated with hanging baskets of pink, yellow, and blue flowers. We walked to the farmhouse. In the living room June opened the drapes of a large picture window. Beyond the pane appeared a breathtaking view of 10,778-foot Mount Baker in Washington's Cascade Range. Closer in, cattle browsed in year-round green fields, and stately fir trees promenaded in a line, partitioning Canada from the United States. Observing the dreamy panorama was like leafing through the pages of a children's picture book.

"The Abbotsford area has grown to about 60,000," June said, adding, "we're getting a lot of commuters from Vancouver. We've always had different nationalities in the valley—Chinese, English, and Scotch. Now we have East Indians who own about 60 percent of the vegetable and berry farms. But here in Fraser Valley most of the dairymen are Dutch."

The first immigrants to cultivate the Fraser encountered great stands of virgin timber that had to be cleared. Eventually, lumbermen began logging operations, built mills, and laid railroad tracks on the northern bank of the Fraser River. Freight trains clamored along the river from mill to mill. Today the forests still echo with the growl and whir of logging equipment. Three-foot-thick logs dangle from crane-like machines called yarder rigs, and the air carries a faint odor of cedar.

(Continued on page 186)

Conductor Henry Reimer and engineer Hugh Campbell check last-minute details before the excursion train Royal Hudson *makes a run north of the Fraser Valley—an area of rich lowlands and forested peaks in British Columbia.*

After breaking up
a log boom on the Stave
River in Ruskin, British
Columbia, Leo Patterson
culls western red cedar
logs with a towline.
The timber will go to a
nearby sawmill, which
will cut the logs into
shakes and shingles.
"I gave up fishing for
logging. Now I wouldn't
want to do anything
else," says Leo, a lifelong
resident of Fraser
Valley. Since the 1930s,
Douglas fir, western
hemlock, and western
red cedar have sustained
the local lumber
industry, an economic
mainstay in the valley.

*O*nce ravaged by floods, fields in Fraser Valley nurture some 865 dairy farms. The valley also produces the highest per-acre yield of raspberries in North America. Curving past farmsteads, a serene channel drifts toward the Fraser. In the 1880s immigrants began to tame this bottomland by building dikes that controlled overflow from the Fraser and its tributaries.

FOLLOWING PAGES: *Forbidding ice walls twist to 80-foot heights above hikers on Matanuska Glacier. Centuries ago, the massive river of ice helped carve Matanuska Valley, the agricultural heartland of Alaska and the fastest growing population area in the state.*

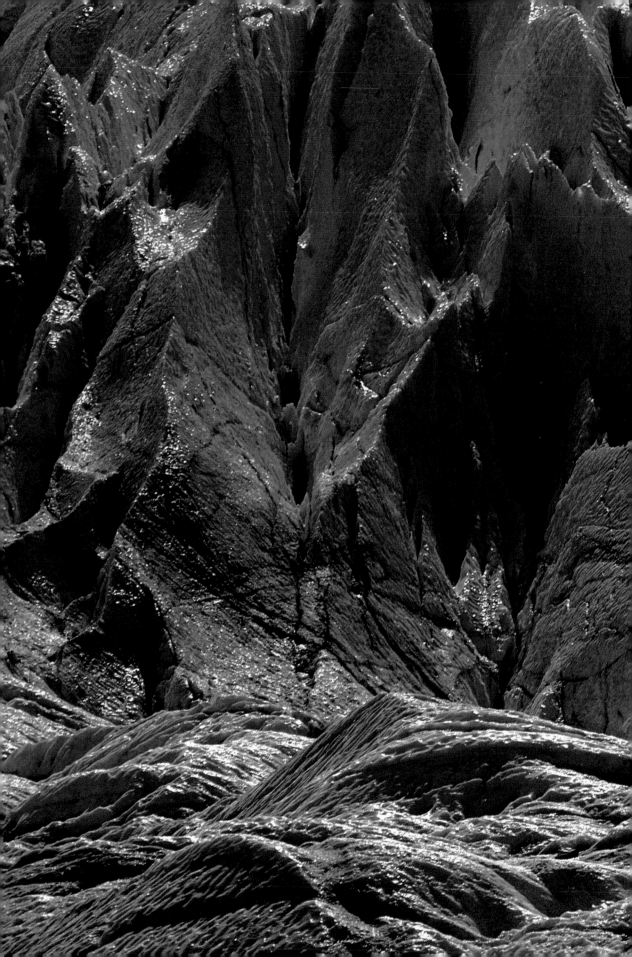

Early one evening as the clouds were dripping mist, I drove east from Vancouver, leaving the more urban western valley behind me, and headed along the Fraser's north shore. The valley seemed to age and slow down as I followed the serpentine highway through a string of towns. Mountain slopes rose steeply to my left, and log booms, waiting to be sorted, hugged the shoreline to my right. It was quitting time at the mills, and men wearing yellow hats and plaid shirts and carrying black lunch pails smiled and waved at me as I passed. After crossing a narrow bridge, I drove down to the water's edge where Leo Patterson was waiting for me.

Leo knows the lumbering business. For 20 years he's been pushing log booms to the mills along the Stave River, which feeds into the Fraser. He can probably tell you more about the Fraser Valley than anyone you would ever meet. Leo can look right out his kitchen window across the river at the farmhouse where he was born. His 89-year-old mother grew up on the other side of the road, and his grandfather was one of the original stampeders who came from California in search of gold. "Altogether," Leo told me in his lilting voice, "my family's been here some 125 years."

The life of a lumberman seems to be a difficult lot, I said. "Sure I have to work hard," Leo replied. "Sometimes seven days a week. And it's rough when I have to break up the ice in the winter. Even so I wouldn't want to do anything else or live any other place. We can get to Vancouver in an hour, and we've got the mountains, the river, and the forests."

I went on the river that evening with Leo and his wife, Eileen, in his tug, the *Canim Clipper*. As the boat churned upriver, cool breezes slapped at my face. I turned to look at a fleet of fishing boats drifting into the reddish, disappearing sun. "Look, now. These are low-grade logs," Leo said, angling alongside them with the skill of a race-car driver. I had to look carefully to see the flaws in the brown, crinkled wood. "A 60-foot section can bring up to $600 per thousand board feet. But you know," he said, "we're just behind the United States in using up all our wood. One of the mills nearby cuts a million feet a week. We've already logged all the timber in this part of the valley. There's still some around Harrison Lake and Chilliwack. But there you're moving into higher country and getting into trees such as hemlock. They tend to be poorer quality above 5,000 feet." Most of the business Leo handles is with small, family-operated mills that are struggling to keep pace with larger ones. "The big mills have such enormous waste," he said. "The small mills depend on me giving them the kind of logs they can handle; I know what they need. That's why it's too bad I don't have an apprentice following me."

Not more than a few miles from where the Pattersons live lies the charming town of Mission. Here, each morning and evening on a steep hillside, the bells of Westminster Abbey toll rhythmically, summoning the Benedictine monks to prayer. Early one morning I drove up the road to the abbey. Already the monks were tilling the soil. Behind the abbey I sat down on a bench and waited to see what had been promised as the most spectacular view in the entire valley.

The fog rolled back like the curtains in a theater, and the pageantry began some 600 feet below me. Taupe sandbars seemed to glide across the water, and toy-size boats bounced in ripples, spouting and spewing. Beyond them miniature white houses rose from the grass like bumps on a square piece of dotted Swiss cloth. Here and there, against the backdrop of purple-hued mountains, silos stood as straight as lean silver bullets. The pinkish morning light draped across the scene as though it were a wispy veil masking the whimsical set of a ballet. The natural drama had fulfilled the promise, and my thoughts turned north to Alaska and a captivating valley called Matanuska.

T Matanuska

he valley gave me a blustery greeting. At times the wind comes roaring down the backsides of the mountains at gusts up to 90 miles an hour, kicking up blinding dust storms. "This valley blew in, and it will probably blow out," residents say. Cottonwoods, alders, and birches sway, their branches snapping and cracking, and leaves swirl in crazy loops and circles. Barn doors creak on rusty hinges; cattle huddle in shelterless fields; rosy-faced children peer from rattling windows. When, at last, the winds subside, the countryside basks in its rejuvenation.

The deep trough known as the Matanuska Valley formed centuries ago. During five successive periods, ice sheets crept down from the Chugach and Talkeetna Mountains and advanced across the valley's present-day site. When the glaciers retreated, they left behind a broad 80-mile-long passageway marked by sparkling lakes, bedrock buttes, and rolling forests and meadows ribboned by silt-laden streams. The Matanuska begins just north of Eklutna, about 30 miles from Anchorage, and reaches northeastward to the Matanuska Glacier, westward to the Susitna River, and southward to Knik along the Knik Arm. Matanuska is the state's agricultural heartland; the valley's fields grow grain, hay, and sometimes outsize vegetables.

One glacial legacy is Bodenburg Butte. On an August afternoon I set out to climb it. Ordinarily, it is a moderate hike, but I was challenged by the startling force of the winds sweeping off the Knik River at about 50 miles an hour. I wound higher along the treeless, fissured rock trail. The wind chided me, trying to propel me backward. Gray loess—the texture of talcum powder—covered me and burrowed into every pore. My face smarted; it felt like a pin cushion being jabbed with hundreds of fine needles. Finally I reached the summit. Bracing myself against the wind, I looked down at the valley. Its floor spread out 881 feet below. The languid, turbid waters of the Matanuska and Knik Rivers mingled to the southwest, then drifted past camelback islands before penetrating the gaping Knik Arm. On the northwest side pale blue walls paraded upriver to the Matanuska Glacier, hidden by a distant bend. Beneath me a muted orange barn stood as conspicuous as a bright pumpkin amid jade fields.

"That bedrock hump you were climbing," U. S. Geological Survey geologist Gary Winkler told me several days later in his office in Anchorage, "is called a *roche moutonnée*, or loosely translated, 'the fleecy back of a sheep.' It's typical for glaciers to try to modify outcrops, but they don't succeed entirely. They just smooth and round them. The glaciers are always busy grinding rock flour." He was referring to the loess that had costumed me as I climbed Bodenburg Butte. Geologists cannot yet pinpoint the exact role the ice sheets played in creating the valley. "Although glaciers covered the area," Gary explained, "a fault system paralleling the valley from east to west made it easier for the ice sheets to quarry along the zone of fractured rock. Local bedrock suggests, too, that the area was already lower than adjacent highlands some 60 to 70 million years ago, long before the Knik and Matanuska Glaciers were formed. When the ice arrived, it simply deepened the valley by grinding out the floor and undercutting the walls."

Emerging from deep within the perpetually snow-robed Chugach Mountains, the Matanuska Glacier extends nearly 28 miles and averages two miles in width. In the last 7,000 years it has fluctuated no more than a mile or two from its present position. Late one afternoon, while the sun still warmed the air in summer's long daylight hours, I hiked onto the ice field. Shadows flitted in and out of shallow, blue-tinged crevasses and caves. Sticky mud pitted with tiny stones oozed around my feet. The aging glacier seemed to chatter to me, and drops of water from melting icicles made my skin tingle. The ice field's architecture was graceful and symmetrical; I admired its bluish spires and obelisk-shaped seracs. The austere beauty of the massive river of ice pleased me, but its awesome power overwhelmed me.

Just as the evolution of the Matanuska Valley area intrigues geologists, so its frontier years absorb historians. Once it was home to Eskimos, some experts believe. Tanaina Indians have lived here for many years. When Russian trappers drifted inland in the early 19th century, they found a region abounding in fox, beaver, and otter. Yet even as the 20th century dawned, only sparse settlements dotted the valley. Then came the cry of gold in the Klondike. Alaska boomed as stampeders rushed in. Later, homesteaders in the valley—joined by disappointed miners—cleared land for farms, a few stores, and a church. One trait identified these pioneers: a willingness to work hard. Activity centered on "sunny Knik, the California of Alaska," a teeming waterfront community along the Knik Arm. By 1916 Knik, bypassed by the railroad, had faded, and farmers had shifted to nearby Palmer and Wasilla. These communities have remained the hub of the valley.

Jim Fox recounts names, dates, and events in the valley's history without even a glance at a book. At 26 he's a published author, as well as a gardener who takes great pride in his English-style flowerbeds. I found him in Palmer one evening as he was returning from a long day in his flower garden.

"The federal government has had a lot to do with Matanuska Valley," he said. "They brought the railroad here in 1916, and when World War II broke out, they built an air base nearby. They also used our coal from the fields east of here. It doesn't stop there," he added. "The oil boom has brought people to Anchorage, and they eventually move out to the valley. We've inherited the title 'bedroom community of Anchorage.' Then, of course, there were the 1935 colonists; my grandparents were among them."

The colonists Jim referred to had been part of a program begun by President Franklin D. Roosevelt during the Depression. Officials looked to the Matanuska's rich, nearly deserted frontier as a place to help reduce the country's swelling relief lines. In turn, they believed, the Alaskan economy would benefit as more food was produced locally. Some 200 families, each allotted a minimum of 40 acres, were brought to Palmer from Minnesota, Wisconsin, and Michigan. By the end of the first year, however, a third of the newcomers had left. Some were too inexperienced in farming, and others were unable to cope with the hardships of living in an isolated wilderness. Those colonists who remained established agriculture in the valley mainly through their perseverance. To make land productive in regions near the Arctic Circle, farmers must overcome eight months of cool temperatures. They must compress their growing season into no more than 120 days.

One struggling farmer is Pat Mulligan. Outside Palmer, Pat works some 240 acres that roll close to the base of Pioneer Peak, a 6,398-foot spire of the Chugach Mountains. The farm's setting is inspirational: blue skies, billowing clouds, and the enduring mountains. As we drove through ripening fields capable of producing 80-pound cabbages in the sun-rich hours of summer, Pat voiced his concern for the future of agriculture. "What we produce right now is going to local markets mostly in Anchorage; it's such a limited market. It's too easy for wholesale buyers in Anchorage to get produce out of the lower forty-eight at the present time. A big problem is getting the message to Anchorage that there's a thriving agricultural community right at its back door. But it's tough getting farmers organized; this is a land of individualists."

We rounded a corner, where a pet moose grazed, and ran into a new problem facing Matanuska farmers. Suburban creep is whittling away the land. Across the road Pat showed me a farm that had recently been subdivided and sold. "We'll never get it back," he said. "Look at Los Angeles. That area used to be some of the best agricultural land around. It's now covered and crowded by subdivisions. Some days you can't even breathe the air down there."

Pat and his wife work hard, and they worry. "The state is trying to encourage people to return to cultivating the land through favorable loan arrangements," Pat said. "Farming builds character; it's just too bad that character can't be used for collateral. We just go from year to year, but I hope we'll be established in ten years. It's so beautiful here; it takes your breath away. The beauty of the valley makes all our struggles worthwhile."

Today, on a percentage basis, the Matanuska Valley is the fastest growing area in Alaska, an official told me. Throughout the summer, tourists, backpackers, and fishermen jam campgrounds and roadways. Yet the region's frontier quality endures. I found it beside a sturdy log cabin, once a homesteader's paradise, but now abandoned and filled with the silence of memories. The cabin hugged a carefree meadow aglow in shocking pink fireweed. An amber light tinted the distant mountains. Though fresh and innocent, the air hinted of fall. September, the harvest month, would soon arrive. Then October snows would blanket the land, and days of darkness would follow. With one lingering gaze, I turned and walked away through the fireweed, heeding a sourdough's oft-repeated words:

> When summer turns to autumn
> And the blueberry leaves are gold
> When fireweed blooms to the end of the stem
> It's time for me to go.

To me the valleys of the Pacific reaches, like all the valleys of North America, are treasure chests: When opened, their beauty and riches dazzle. Though development encroaches on many of them, these lands retain their grandeur and the spirit of their earliest settlers. It's as though nature, recognizing the preciousness of her valleys, had tucked them safely away between vast mountain ranges where she could nurture them for all time.

Strewn with flowering yarrow, Bodenburg Butte overlooks the southeastern stretch of the Matanuska Valley. Thick forests, including conifers and birch, *once covered this land where crops of hay, barley, and vegetables now grow. Above the silt-laden Knik River, clouds on the Chugach Mountains drape peaks known locally as the Three Sisters.*

Monument to settlers, a barn dates back to the Matanuska Colony, a group of midwestern families who came to the valley in 1935. The colonists received land under a federal program drafted to aid farmers during the Great Depression. The hardships of pioneer life in Matanuska drove many of the newcomers away. Most of those who stayed eventually made the valley productive. Modern-day settler Pat Mulligan (right) harvests cauliflower beneath Pioneer Peak.

FOLLOWING PAGES: A deserted log cabin in a meadow glowing with fireweed captures the frontier flavor of Matanuska. The valley lies less than an hour's drive from Anchorage. As the city's population grows, the subdivision of valley land to build bedroom communities imperils Matanuska's wilderness splendor.

Notes on Contributors

Hawaii-born photographer RICHARD A. COOKE III has covered varied free-lance assignments for the National Geographic Society, including *Canada's Wilderness Lands* and *America's Wild and Scenic Rivers* for Special Publications. His photographs have also appeared in such magazines as *Outside* and *Sports Afield*.

TONI EUGENE, an English major who graduated from Gettysburg College, joined the Society's staff in 1971. She has written picture captions for numerous Special Publications. Before her *Valleys* assignment, she wrote a chapter for *America's Wild and Scenic Rivers*. She is the author of the Special Publications children's book *Strange Animals of Australia*.

During the past two decades free-lance photographer LOWELL GEORGIA has covered more than 65 assignments for the Society, including *Journey into China*. He photographed *Into the Wilderness* and has contributed to other Special Publications, including *America's Hidden Corners* and *The Craftsman in America*.

After covering the war in Vietnam for the Associated Press, MARK GODFREY stayed in Asia as a contract photographer for *Life*. His photographic work for Special Publications includes *The Mighty Aztecs*, *Exploring America's Backcountry*, and *Frontiers of Science*.

DAVID HISER, a free-lance photographer who speaks fluent Spanish, was a natural choice to send to Mexico for *Valleys*. He contributed to the Special Publication *Splendors of the Past* and has taken numerous photographs for NATIONAL GEOGRAPHIC articles.

Staff member CHRISTINE ECKSTROM LEE, a resident of Arlington, Virginia, has journeyed often to the nearby Shenandoah Valley on hiking, fishing, and canoeing trips. The coauthor of the Special Publication *America's Atlantic Isles*, she also wrote a chapter for *Isles of the Caribbean* and contributed to the Society's *Peoples and Places of the Past*.

JANE R. MCCAULEY lived three years in Geneva, Switzerland, before joining the Society's staff in 1970. Her writing credits for Special Publications include numerous picture captions, two Books for Young Explorers— *Ways Animals Sleep* and *Baby Birds and How They Grow*—and a chapter on Afghanistan for the Special Publication *Secret Corners of the World*.

The *Valleys* assignment took staff member H. ROBERT MORRISON to the Great Plains, a region he had visited for the Special Publication *Preserving America's Past*. His many contributions to Special Publications include *Mysteries of the Ancient World* and *America's Majestic Canyons*. He is the coauthor of the Special Publication *America's Atlantic Isles*.

Graduate studies in art history and archaeology lured staff writer GENE S. STUART to the Yucatán Peninsula in Mexico, where she and her archaeologist husband lived and worked for several years. Her narratives about the Southwest and Mexico appear in the Special Publications *The Mysterious Maya*, *The Mighty Aztecs*, and *Preserving America's Past*.

TIM THOMPSON, who began his career as a writer, became a full-time photographer in 1972. His photographs have appeared in *Time-Life* books, *Audubon*, and various airline magazines. He contributed to the Special Publication *Alaska's Magnificent Parklands*.

LOWELL GEORGIA

Delicate blossom of a day lily blushes in the morning sun of Alabama's Wills Valley. The flower will die before sunset, having lived but a few hours. New buds will bloom and wither with each day of summer. Originally a cultivated species, the day lily now grows wild, decorating meadows and wooded hillsides in many of America's valleys.

Composition for *Exploring America's Valleys: From the Shenandoah to the Rio Grande* by National Geographic's Photographic Services, Carl M. Shrader, Director, Lawrence F. Ludwig, Assistant Director. Printed and bound by Kingsport Press, Kingsport, Tennessee. Film preparation by Catharine Cooke Studio, Inc., New York, New York. Color separations by the Lanman Progressive Co., Washington, D.C.; Lincoln Graphics, Inc., Cherry Hill, New Jersey; and NEC, Inc., Nashville, Tennessee.

Library of Congress CIP Data
Main entry under title:
Exploring America's valleys.
   Bibliography: p.
   Includes index.
   1. Valleys—United States. I. National Geographic Society (U.S.). Special Publications Division.
GB564.E96 1984   917.30944   84-6804
ISBN 0-87044-476-X (regular edition)
ISBN 0-87044-481-6 (library edition)

Index

Boldface indicates illustrations.
Italic indicates illustration captions.

Afton, Wyo. 85, 87; winter racing
  94-95
Alabama *see* Wills Valley
Alabama (band) 37, 38; benefit concerts
  37, 44-45
Alaska *see* Matanuska Valley
Aluminum refinery: Jonquière,
  Quebec 15
American Revolution 13, 23
Amish: Kickapoo Valley, Wis. 57-58
Ancient Bristlecone Pine Forest,
  Calif. 167
Anderson, Mel 108
Anse St-Jean, Quebec 16
Apache 147-148
Apple orchards: Virginia 24, *25*, 36
Arizona *see* Verde Valley
Arkansas *see* Arkansas Valley
Arkansas Valley, Ark. *63*, 69-71, 74;
  aerial view 63-64
ARVAC Rural Folk Crafts *69*, 70-71
Aspen, quaking 88-89
Austin, Chet 70
Austin, Mary: quoted *173*, 175, 177
Aztecs 137

Bailey, Carlos 37
Banta, Jerry 76
Barron, Mel 85
Basques 105, 107
Battle of New Market: reenactment
  28-29, 30-31, 35
Beckman, Jack 122
Beecher, Henry Ward *see* What
  rè Sama
Belugas: St. Lawrence River, Canada
  13, 16, 22
Berry, Edwin *153*, 155
Beulah Baptist Church, Fyffe, Ala.
  37, 43
Bicycle trail: Wisconsin 58, 69
Blue Ridge Mountains, Va. 24-25, 32-33
Bodenburg Butte, Alaska 187, 190-191
Bonneville, Lake (prehistoric) 92
Bonney, William H. (Billy the Kid) 147
Bouchard, Diane 15
Boudreault, Hervé 17
Boudreault, Nazaire 16, 21
Bough, Dennis and June 50
Buchholz, Duane 176
Bureau of Land Management: grazing
  control 93, 104-105
Bye, Erik 57
Byington, Evert K. 70

California *see* Owens Valley
Campbell, Hugh 179
Canada *see* Fraser Valley;
  Saguenay Valley

"caribou" (drink) 15, *19*
Carnaval Souvenir, Chicoutimi, Quebec
  13-15, 17; cancan 18-19
Carney, Dan 25
Carter, Mont.: grain elevators 54-55
Cartier, Jacques 13
Caso, Alfonso 137
Cathedral Rock, Ariz. 120
Cattle *see* Dairy farming; Ranching
Centre Linguistique, Jonquière,
  Quebec 15
Cerro Gordo mine, Inyo Mountains 175
Cha-lipun, Chief 124; surrender 124
Cherokee Indians 36-37
Chichimec Indians: conquest 139, 140
Chicoutimi, Quebec: winter festival
  13-15, 17; cancan 18-19
Chimney Rock, Nebr. 46-47, *49*, 75
Christensen, Ray 92
Christiansen, Paige 148
Civil War, U. S.: Virginia battles 25,
  25, reenactment 28-29, 30-31, 35, *35*
Clark, William 49
Cleopatra Hill, Ariz. 126-127; mines
  123, 126
Cliff dwellings: Arizona 118-119,
  121, 122
Cliffs of Rome (buttes), Oreg. 93, *111*,
  112-113
Contreras, Luz María 140
Convent of the Cross, Mexico 140; cell
  141
Copper 106, *117*, *126*
Cortés, Hernán 137
Coyotes: sheep kills 108
Cranney, King 90
Crook, George 124
Currie, Nev. 116-117

Dairy farming: Fraser Valley,
  British Columbia 182-183; Kickapoo
  Valley, Wis. *71*, 72-73; Star Valley,
  Wyo. 85-86, 87
Dancers: Chicoutimi, Quebec 18-19;
  Oaxaca, Mexico 136
DeDecker, Mary 176
de las Casas, Ignacio Mariano 139-140
Dogwood blossoms 32-33
Driftless Area (geologic zone) 56-57
Dyes, natural 138

Egan, Howard and Richard
  Erastus 106
Eiguren, Fred 105
Elephant Butte Reservoir, N. Mex. 148
Elk: California 166; Wyoming 86
Ely, Nev. 106, 107
Erickson, Bart 86
Espejo, Antonio de 123

Farming 57, 58, *71*, 72-73, 75-76,
  76, 77-78, 178, 182-183, 187-189,
  190-191, 192
Field, Jo Ann 91
Fillmore, Kay and Ralph 104
Fjord 12, 15-16
Flint, Roy K. 23
Fort Benton, Mont. 51
Fort Langley National Historic Park,

British Columbia 177-178
Fort Payne, Ala. 37, *44*
Fort Selden, N. Mex. 148
Fort Smith, Ark. 71, 74; court 66, 67
Fort Verde, Ariz. 124
Fox, Jim 188
Fraser, Simon 177
Fraser Valley, British Columbia
  156-157, 177-178, 186-187; agriculture
  178, *182*, dairy farms 182-183;
  history 177-178; logging 178, 180-181,
  181, 186
Fur trading: Saguenay Valley,
  Quebec 14
Furumoto, Augustine 159

Gallegos, Albert 149
García Blanco, Luis, and son 130-131
Gardner, Ada 87
Gardner, Low 86-87
Garner, Nathan 25
Geronimo (Apache chief) 148
Goldfinch 77
Gould, Jay: mansion 22, 39
Government Palace, Querétaro, Mexico
  142-143
Great Falls, Mont. 49, 50, 51
Great Salt Lake, Utah 90; salt content
  92; waterfowl 102-103
Greater Vancouver, British Columbia:
  population 177
Grief Hill, Ariz. 121, 124

Haas, Stan 75-76
Hale, Ted 87
Hanging Judge *see* Parker, Isaac C.
Hanley, Judi and Mike 104
Harper's Ferry, W. Va. 24; aerial
  view 34
Hawaii *see* Kohala (region)
Heliographs 148
Helland, Selmer 50
Hind, John 160
Holden, Thora 57
Honokane Iki Valley, Hawaii 159, 161,
  164-165
Hoopes, Royce, and family *87*, 88-89
House of the Dogs, Querétaro, Mexico
  139-140
Howard, Elizabeth 37
Howard, Gordon *60*, 74, 75, 76
Howard, Patty 61, 74
Hudson, Henry 22
Hudson River, N.Y. 10-11, 22, 23-24
Hudson Valley, N.Y. 10-11, 13, 22-24;
  mansions 22, 39; settlers 22
Hudson's Bay Company 14, 178
Hunsaker, Mary Stewart 100
Huron Indians 13

Irises, wild 174
Irving, Washington 22-23; study 40
Ivey, Gene 43

Jackson, "Stonewall" 25
Jakes Valley, Nev.: sheep 107
Jerome, Ariz. 123-124, 126-127;
  restoration 123, *126*

Jiménez, Manuel 138
Jonquière, Quebec 14, 15
Jordan, Michael 92
Jordan Valley, Oreg. 92-93, 104-106;
  gold mining 92, 105; grazing 92-93,
  104; ranching 105, 109; rodeo 105-106,
  110-111
Jornada del Muerto (Journey of Death)
  147, 148, 149, 150-151
Joy, A. Z. 106-107
Juárez, Benito 140, 140

Kamehameha I, King (Hawaiian
  Islands) 159, 161
Kearsarge mine, Calif. 175
Kempf, William 57-58
Kennecott Copper Corporation 106
Kickapoo Valley, Wis. 56-58, 69; aerial
  view 78-79; Amish 57-58; contour
  plowing 76, 78-79; dairy farming 71,
  72-73; Norwegians 57, 80; settlement
  57
Kohala (region), Hawaii 159, 159; cliffs
  158; myths 160; valleys 159-162
Kohala Ditch Trail 160, 165

Lacey Ranch, Calif. 170
Lawrence, D. H.: quoted 137
Leblanc, Serge 15
The Legend of Sleepy Hollow (Irving):
  quoted 22
Lequerica, Tim 105
Lewis, Meriwether 49
Lile, Jimmy 71
Loarca, Eduardo 146
Lorang, Dennis 55
Los Angeles aqueduct, Calif. 176-177
Louisiana Purchase (1803) 49
Lunes de Cerro (festival) 136
Lyndhurst (mansion), Tarrytown,
  N.Y. 39

McReynolds, Harry 87
Madariaga, Richard and Sheila 104
Magoffin, Susan Shelby 147
Mairs, Glorian and Omie 175
Malmstrom Air Force Base, Mont.
  50-51
Maple syrup process 58
Matanuska Glacier, Alaska 184-185,
  187-188
Matanuska Valley, Alaska 187-189;
  agriculture 187, 188-189, 190-191,
  192, 193, 194-195; settlement 188
Matteri, Jim 104
Maximilian, Emperor (Mexico) 140,
  140; cell 141
Meadowlark, western 63
Mesilla, N. Mex. 147
Mexico: territory ceded to U. S. 121,
  145, 146; see also Middle Rio Grande
  Valley; Oaxaca, Valley of; Querétaro
  (valley)
Middle Rio Grande Valley, N. Mex.
  146-149; cultural mix 147; religious
  customs 149; settlement 147
Miles, Nelson A. 148
Mission, British Columbia: Benedictine
  abbey 186

Missouri Breaks (rock formations),
  Mont. 51, 56
Missouri River, Mont.: course changes
  51, 56; falls 48, 49, 50
Missouri Valley, Mont. 48-56; aerial
  view 52-53; agriculture 50, 51, 52-55;
  missiles 50-51
Mixtec Indians: gold pectoral 134, 137
Montana see Missouri Valley
Montaño Sanchez, José 138
Monte Albán, Mexico 134-135, 137
Montezuma Castle (cliff dwelling),
  Ariz. 119, 121
Montezuma Well (ruins), Ariz. 122
Mormon Tabernacle, Salt Lake City,
  Utah 91; choir 91, 100-101
Mormons 75, 90-91; polygamy 90
Morton salt factory: Utah 92
Mule-ears (wild flowers) 84
Mulligan, Pat 189, 193
Mustangs: Nevada 82-83, 85, 106-107

Ndé Ndé-z (Apache chief) 123
Nebraska see North Platte Valley
Nelson, Ron 56-57
Nevada see Jakes Valley; Steptoe
  Valley
Nevada Consolidated Copper
  Company 106
New Mexico see Rio Grande
  Valley (middle)
New York see Hudson Valley
Nichols, Guy 74
North Platte Valley, Nebr. 46-47, 49,
  62-63, 74-76; agriculture 75-76;
  wagon-train trek 59, 60-61, 74-75
Norwegian settlers: Kickapoo Valley,
  Wis. 57, 80

Oak Creek, Ariz. 120
Oaxaca (city), Mexico: cathedral 128;
  Church of Santo Domingo 129;
  market 137
Oaxaca, Valley of, Mexico 124, 137-139;
  cultural mix 137; history 128
Oklahoma 66, 69, 74
Oñate, Juan de 146, 147
Oregon see Jordan Valley
Oregon Trail 58, 60-61, 75, 76, 90
Ortiz de Domínguez, Josefa 140,
  142-143, 143
Otomí Indians 139
Ott, Bill 43
Ouachita Mountains, Ark. 69, 70, 74
Ouellet, Francine 14-15
Owen, Randy 37, 38, 44
Owens River, Calif.: diversion 176
Owens Valley, Calif.: 159, 162, 172,
  173, 175-177; aerial view 168-169;
  agriculture 175, cattle raising 170-
  171; tule elk 166, 177; water
  controversy 176-177; wildlife 177
Owyhee River, Oreg. 92, 93, 111,
  112-113
Ozark Mountains, Ark. 69, 70, 71, 74

Padilla, Wanda 122-123
Paiute Indians 106; legend 162
Parker, Isaac C. 66, 71, 74; courtroom

67; death sentences pronounced 66, 74
Patterson, Eileen 186
Patterson, Leo 180, 186
Payne, Capt. John 37
Pelicans, white 102-103
Penitentes (religious sect) 149, 153
Petit Jean (mountain), Ark. 69
Philipsburg (mansion), North
  Tarrytown, N.Y. 22
Pohanka, Brian 35
Pololu Valley, Hawaii 159, 163
Potomac River, U. S.: confluence
  with Shenandoah 24, 34
Potters: Oaxaca, Valley of, Mexico
  130-131
Powers, Madge 71
Pueblo Indians 147
Pueblos: Arizona 122, 125

Querétaro (city), Mexico 144-145;
  aqueduct 144-145; architecture
  139-140, Government Palace 142-143
Querétaro (valley), Mexico 139-140, 146
Quilting 68, 71

Rainbow Falls, Mont. 48
Ranching: Jordan Valley, Oreg.
  104-105, 109, grazing 92-93, 104;
  Owens Valley, Calif. 170, 175; Star
  Valley, Wyo. 90; Steptoe Valley,
  Nev. 107-108, 114-116
Reeves, Maggie 86
Reeves, Stanley 85-86
Reid, Byron L. 37
Reimer, Henry 178
Rio Grande Valley (middle), N. Mex.
  146-149; cultural mix 147; religious
  customs 149; settlement 146-147
Rockefeller, Winthrop 69, 70
Rocky Mountains, Canada-U. S.
  49-50, 85
Ross, June 178
Royal Hudson (train) 179
Russell, D. K. 36
Russell, Robert 36
Ruth, Nev.: copper mine 106, 117

Saguenay River, Quebec 12, 13, 15-16;
  source 15, 20
Saguenay Valley, Quebec 13-22;
  agriculture 16, 21; French Canadians
  13-16; industry 14, 20; language 15
St-Hilaire, Marc 14
St-Jean, Guy 15
St. Lawrence River, Canada 13, 15, 16
Salmon, "Sam" 71
Salt Lake City, Utah 85, 90; floods
  91-92
Salt Lake Valley, Utah 90-92, 99; skiing
  91, 98; tourism 91
Salt River Range, Wyo. 85, 86, 96-97
Saltair (salt factory) 92
Salvi, Joe 108
Sanchez, Gil and Priscilla 149
San Fernando Valley, Calif.:
  irrigation 176
San Francisco Javier (hacienda),
  Mexico 131, 132-133
Santo Domingo, Church of,

Oaxaca, Mexico **129**
Schellbourne, Nev. 106
Scotts Bluff National Monument, Nebr. 76
Seeman, Edna **68**, 71
Sequoyah (Cherokee Indian) 36
Serra, Junípero 140
Shape-note singing 37-38
Sheep raising: 104-105, 107-108, **114-115;** shearing 107, **114-115**
Shenandoah National Park, Va. 25; bear study 25; established *32*
Shenandoah River, Va.-W.Va.: confluence with Potomac 24, **34**
Shenandoah Valley, Va.-W.Va. 13, 24-36; aerial view **26-27;** agriculture *25*, 35-36; Civil War 25, *29*, 35; settlement 24, *32*
Skiing **80-81**, 91, **98-99**
Skinner, Bob, Jr. 93
Skinner, Bob, Sr. 92-93
Skinner, Silas 92
Smith, Bernard 58
Smith, Gus 37
Snowbird Ski Resort, Utah 91, **98**
Snowmobiling 87
Socorro, N. Mex. 147, 148
Soderling, Rene 70
Soldiers Grove (town), Wis.: solar heating 58
Spanish exploration: New World 9, 123, 137, 139, 146-147
Sproat, Cheri 160-162
Sproat, Clyde 160-162, **165**
Star Valley, Wyo. 84-90; dairy farming 85-86; hunting 86-87; Mormons 90; recreation 87, **94-95**
Star Valley Cheese Cooperative, Thayne, Wyo. 86
Steffensmeier, "Wild Bill" **59**
Steptoe Valley, Nev. 106-108; copper mining 106, *117;* ranching 107-108; sheep shearing 107, **115**
Stuart, Jim 25
Sunnyside (home), Tarrytown, N.Y. 22, *41;* study 40

Tabernacle, Salt Lake City, Utah 91, **100-101**
Taylor Grazing Act 93, 104-105
Teotitlán del Valle, Mexico 137-138
Textile industry: Oaxaca, Mexico 137-138
Thatcher, Moses 90
Tomb 7, Monte Albán, Oaxaca, Mexico 137
Tonto Apache 122; creation myth 122
Trail of Tears 37
Treaty of Guadalupe Hidalgo *145*, 146
Tuzigoot (pueblo), Ariz. 124, **125**
Twain, Mark 51

Uhalde, Gracian and Rena 107-108
U. S.-Mexican War: treaty ending *145*, 146
Utah *see* Salt Lake Valley

Valdez Mora, Rodolfo 146
Vale Project 93

Val-Jalbert, Quebec: pulp mill **20**
Van Cortlandt Manor, Croton-on-Hudson, N.Y. 22; kitchen **41**
Verde Valley, Ariz. 121-124; mining 123; pioneers 121; wildlife 122
Villa del Pueblito, Mexico 140; legends 146
Villanueva, Norman L. 51
Virginia *see* Shenandoah Valley
Virginia Military Institute, Lexington, Va. *29*, 35
Vitale, Lou 70

Wagon trains 74-75; re-creation **59**, **60-61,** 74-76
West Point, N.Y. *13;* fortifications, Revolutionary War 23
Westby, Wis.: Norwegian community 57; ski jumping 80-81
What rè Sama (Apache Indian) 123
Wheat farming: Montana 50, *51*, **52-53,** *54*,
White Cliffs (region), Mont. 51; aerial view **52-53**

Whitfield, Bill **109**
Wilcox, Martha 41
Wilkes, Bart 87, 90
Wills Valley, Ala. 13, 36-38; aerial view **42;** Cherokee Indians 36-37; musical traditions 37-38, **43**
Winkler, Gary 187-188
Winneduma Rock, Calif. 162; legend 162
Winrock International: animal husbandry studies 69-70
Wisconsin *see* Kickapoo Valley
Wyoming *see* Star Valley

Yarrow 190-191
Yazman, Jim 70
Yellow-spine thistle **62**
Young, Brigham 75, 90, *101*
Yucca **152**
Yusko, Gordon 178

Zapotec civilization 124, *135*, 137; mountaintop city **134-135,** 137

Acknowledgments

The Special Publications Division is grateful to the individuals, groups, and organizations named and quoted in the text and to those cited here for their assistance during the preparation of this book.

Throughout: DR. WILLIAM V. SLITER; The Smithsonian Institution

Chapter 1: Archive of Folk Culture: The Library of Congress; WILLIAM H. BORDERS, JR., DENNIS CARTER, GEORGIA MACLEAN; New Market Battlefield Park; LOUIS B. PARENT, GERALD E. PARSONS. **Chapter 2:** THOMAS J. CROWSON, THOMAS R. DOERING, DR. JOHN JANOVY, JR., JOANN M. KYRAL, JOHN G. LEPLEY, DR. M. K. McCARTY, JAMES O. RADKE. **Chapter 3:** MAX M. BLACKHAM, GRACE HYDE, BARRY ROSE, TIMOTHY G. STREBEL. **Chapter 4:** DR. DONALD L. BROCKINGTON, DR. FRANK E. KOTTLOWSKI, JOHN MONAGHAN, TED STANS, DR. MARCUS WINTER. **Chapter 5:** RAY SCHAAF, DONALD H. TALMAGE.

Additional Reading

The reader may wish to consult the *National Geographic Index* for pertinent articles, and to refer to the following:
Fernando Benítez, *The Century After Cortés;* William A. Douglass and Jon Bilbao, *Amerikanuak: Basques in the New World;* Mike Hanley with Ellis Lucia, *Owyhee Trails;* Michael P. Malone and Richard B. Roeder, *Montana: A History of Two Centuries;* Kathleen D. Mellen, *The Lonely Warrior: The Life and Times of Kamehameha the Great of Hawaii;* Merrill J. Mattes, *The Great Platte River Road;* Orlando W. Miller, *The Frontier in Alaska and the Matanuska Colony;* Paul C. Phillips, *The Fur Trade;* Genny Schumacher Smith (editor), *Deepest Valley: A Guide to Owens Valley;* C. L. Sonnichsen, *Pass of the North: Four Centuries on the Rio Grande;* John Paddock (editor), *Ancient Oaxaca;* Marta Weigle, *Brothers of Light, Brothers of Blood: The Penitentes of the Southwest;* Joseph W. Whitecotton, *The Zapotecs.*

Additional Music

The reader may wish to consult recordings produced by the National Geographic Society, including: *Cowboy Songs, Songs of the Civil War, Songs of Hawaii, Songs and Sounds of the Sea.*
The reader may also wish to refer to the following: Alabama, *Alabama;* Joan Baez, *Gracias a la Vida;* Mahalia Jackson, *America's Favorite Hymns;* Kate and Anna McGarrigle, *Entre la Jeunesse et la Sagesse;* Mormon Tabernacle Choir, *This Land is Your Land;* Riders in the Sky, *Prairie Serenade;* Stan Rogers, *From Fresh Water;* Sons of the Pioneers, *Tumbleweed Trails.*

Music Credits

Page 23: "The shantyman leads a drearisome life," reprinted from *The Hudson* by Carl Carmer, (c) 1968. **Page 24:** "Shenandoah," words adapted by John A. and Alan Lomax, reprinted from *Folk Song U.S.A.,* Alan Lomax, editor, (c) 1947. **Page 25:** "The Bonnie Blue Flag," words by Harry Macarthy, (c) 1861. **Page 36:** "My Home's in Alabama" by Randy Owen and Teddy Gentry, (c) 1980 Millhouse Music, BMI. Used with permission. **Page 37:** "Dixie Boy" by Jim McBride, (c) 1983 April Music, Inc., and Widmont Music. Administered by April Music, Inc. Used with permission; "Amazing Grace," reprinted from the *U. S. Forces Book of Worship,* (c) 1974. **Page 38:** "Were You There," reprinted from *Old Plantation Hymns* collected by William E. Barton, (c) 1899.

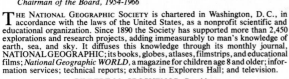